ETHNOSTATISTICS:
Qualitative Foundations for Quantitative Research

ROBERT P. GEPHART, Jr.
University of Alberta, Edmonton

Qualitative Research Methods,
Volume 12

SAGE PUBLICATIONS
The Publishers of Professional Social Science
Newbury Park   Beverly Hills   London   New Delhi

For information address:

SAGE Publications, Inc.
2111 West Hillcrest Drive
Newbury Park, California 91320

SAGE Publications Inc.   SAGE Publications Ltd.
275 South Beverly Drive   28 Banner Street
Beverly Hills   London EC1Y 8QE
California 90212   England

SAGE PUBLICATIONS India Pvt. Ltd.
M-32 Market
Greater Kailash I
New Delhi 110 048 India

Printed in the United States of America

Library of Congress Cataloging-in-Publication Data

Gephart, Robert P., Jr.
  Ethnostatistics: qualitative foundations for quantitative
research.

  (Qualitative research methods; v. 12)
  Bibliography: p.
  1. Social sciences—Statistical methods.   I. Title.
II. Series.
HA29.G45 1988 300′.1′5195 87-26606
ISBN 0-8039-3025-9
ISBN 0-8039-3026-7 (pbk.)

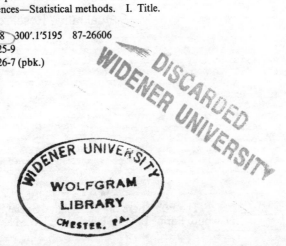

CONTENTS

EDITORS' INTRODUCTION

Statistics are everywhere. Averages, ratios, means, modes, medians, and tests of significance and best fit are now part of our everyday discourse, and these statistics seemingly threaten to bury us under their sheer weight. Social science contributes a good deal to the proliferation of statistics, but it contributes relatively little to the understanding of just how such statistics are produced and used by their makers and consumers. Technical experts take up some of the slack by showing us the proper formulation and application of statistical methods, but these same experts are often at a loss when it comes to describing just how their formal methods are actually put into play and given meaning by those who make use of them.

Ethnostatistics is a clumsy but nonetheless accurate term for denoting the study of the social production and use of statistics. It is the term selected by Robert P. Gephart in Volume 12 of the Sage Series on Qualitative Research Methods to mark three distinct areas of investigation. There is nothing magical about these three areas, but they do offer a beginning classification for what may eventually become a spirited and practical field of social study. In Gephart's scheme, ethnostatistics involves one or more of the following research activities: (1) conducting ethnographic studies of groups that routinely produce statistics, (2) testing the technical and operational assumptions that are involved in the production of statistics, and (3) examining the use of statistics as a rhetorical device in various kinds of research publications.

Each of these domains represents relatively new topical materials for qualitative researchers. Each domain also presumes the emergence of a fairly high level of technical expertise among those who pursue such studies. And each domain requires rather different research methods and theoretical frameworks with which to approach the topics of interest. These areas of study are complex and require a good deal of traditional statistical training but, as Gephart's examples demonstrate, the results are well worth the researcher's efforts.

In a sense, ethnostatistics is another in a long line of attempts to

6

bridge the gap between qualitative and quantitative research. It is, perhaps, a more sophisticated attempt than many because it suggests that this gap can be narrowed only when the methods developed by members of one camp are made use of by members of the other. It argues for the development of a user's (native's) appreciation for the doing of statistics on the part of the researcher, an appreciation that it is neither derogatory nor celebratory. At the same time, it argues for more openness and explication of the part of statistical users such that the influence of their often artful judgments on the results they produce can be more clearly seen. This is a tall order, to be sure, but, given the current questioning of the appropriateness of many statistical routines, it is a timely one.

John Van Maanen
Peter K. Manning
Marc L. Miller

ACKNOWLEDGMENTS

This volume reflects more than a decade of academic endeavors. The original inspiration derives from a statistics course instructed by the late Professor Sanford M. Labovitz, Department of Sociology, University of Calgary, in 1973. The ideas took clearer form in subsequent years when I was variously a student (the University of British Columbia), faculty member (the University of Alberta) and visiting scholar (Massachusetts Institute of Technology). I would like to acknowledge the general support and stimulation provided by these institutions, as well as the comments, criticisms, and/or encouragement I received from a number of scholars: Roy Turner, Carl Sarndal, Peter Frost, Vance Mitchell, Karl Weick, Meryl Louis, Prem Talwar, Dave Jobson, Michael Lynch, Debbie Gladstein, C. R. (Bob) Hinings, Alan Murray, Alan Richardson, Mansour Javidan, Zvi Maimon, Yonhatin Reschef, J. J. Williams, and Brian Bemmels. Blame me, not them, for any troublesome aspects of this manuscript.

John Van Maanen has provided inspiration, comments, and encouragement on my "quantitative projects" for many years now, and has been a mentor, colleague, and friend in innumerable ways. Without his guidance and support, this volume would never have been written. Finally, Bev Zubot and Keith Zubot-Gephart lived through this manuscript, and can tell their own tales of the field. Thus I dedicate the manuscript to Bev and Keith, a labor of love for all their support.

ETHNOSTATISTICS
Qualitative Foundations for Quantitative Research

ROBERT P. GEPHART, Jr.
University of Alberta

1. THE DOMAIN OF ETHNOSTATISTICS

> It is pointless any longer to doubt that an immense, hitherto unknown
> domain of social phenomena has been uncovered [Garfinkel, 1967: ix].

The allure of numbers swept through the human sciences in the late
nineteenth century, bringing "the faith that rigorous measurement could
guarantee irrefutable precision, and might mark the transition between
subjective speculation and a true science" (Gould, 1981: 74). This
"quantifying enthusiasm" (McCloskey, 1985: 7) has left its mark on
social science in the tacit endorsement of Lord Kelvin's dictum: "When
you cannot measure it, when you cannot express it in numbers, your
knowledge is of a meager and unsatisfactory kind" (in McCloskey,
1985: 54).

Thus since Durkheim's (1967) classic analysis of suicide social
scientists have routinely attempted to measure social facts by "assigning
numbers to observations according to some set of rules" (Summers,
1970: 1). Quantitative research and measurement have been proclaimed
as superior ways of producing knowledge (Sellitz and Cook, 1976;
Rudner, 1966; Nachmias and Nachmias, 1976). Commonsense methods
for acquiring knowledge have been widely regarded as unsystematic,
irreplicable, and invalid, and have been displaced in social science by
natural science methods, especially statistics. In this manner, statistical

8

procedures and quantitative methods held an almost monopolistic grip on social science until recent years (Van Maanen, 1979).

The research methods discussed in this volume have played a significant role in the emergence of an alternative rhetoric of quantification in social science.

> Numbers suggest, constrain, and refute; they do not, by themselves, specify the content of scientific theories. Theories are built upon the interpretation of numbers, and interpreters . . . trapped in their own rhetoric . . . fail to discern the prejudice that leads them to one interpretation among many consistent with the numbers [Gould, 1981: 74].

The purposes of this volume are both critical and positive. The critical goal is to discuss methods used to systematically explicate problems in the socially contexted use(s) of statistics. The methods can be used to dereify statistical artifacts and thwart the substitution of methods for theory. The volume does not reject the use of statistics, but rather it suggests methods for studying and improving the uses and meanings of statistics in social research. Criticisms of the uses and misuses of statistics provide necessary rationales for developing alternative techniques.

The present volume is concerned with how to do social research on the use of statistics in quantitative social research; it outlines a program of research on ethnostatistics. Here, I define *ethnostatistics* as the study of the construction, interpretation, and display of statistics in quantitative social research. The monograph displays through example how ethnostatistics can go to work in three areas: studying the production of statistics, statistics at work, and statistics as rhetoric. In addition, it discusses practical and theoretical bases and implications of these three areas of ethnostatistics.

The nature of ethnostatistics can be made clearer by distinguishing it from statistics. *Statistics* has several meanings. First, it is a professional field of inquiry concerned with "the theories and techniques (both descriptive and inferential) that have been developed to manipulate data" (Labovitz and Hagedorn, 1971: 65). Statistics is thus the occupational home of professional statisticians. Statisticians, for present purposes, are seen to include not only scholars employed in departments of statistics, but also social, administrative, and other scientists (in universities and elsewhere) who are concerned with teaching, developing, improving, and using statistical procedures. Second, statistics is a label for certain techniques or rule-governed procedures for doing certain calculations, such as the procedures involved in calculating an analysis of variance. Third, statistics refers to almost any numerical summary that is the outcome of the application of rule-governed calculations. For example, the F ratio, a chi-square value, or the number of runs batted in during a baseball game are statistics in this meaning of the term.

Statistics are used in research to describe and assess relations among observations or variables (Labovitz and Hagedorn, 1971), and statistical issues are important at virtually all points in the quantitative research process. In general, statistical issues concern the technical appropriateness and propriety of procedures selected and used. "Statistics is aimed at better counting, with precise methods of aggregating data, and with estimation" (Bogdan and Ksander, 1980: 302). For example, statistical concerns would include the size of the sample, the correctness of computations, the appropriateness of the statistic to the type of questions posed in the research, and the extent to which the data meet assumptions underlying the statistic (Blalock, 1972). The statistical perspective necessarily emphasizes technical features of the research process. Yet, as statisticians are well aware, resolution of many issues (e.g., the role of replication in inference) is not purely a mathematical or statistical issue: "The actual behavior of scientists must be taken into account" (Guttman, 1977: 25).

Thus it is useful to propose the term *ethnostatistics* to refer to the study of how statistics are actually constructed and used, particularly in scientific research. The prefix *ethno* suggests a concern for the actual behavior, and the informal subcultural, folk, or ethnic knowledge and activities of statistics producers and users. This informal knowledge complements and extends the formal, codified technical knowledge involved in statistics. Ethnostatistics is concerned with the mundane, everyday life practices, and the lay and professional knowledge necessary to implement and use statistics. Ethnostatistics addresses sense-making or interpretive practices (Garfinkel, 1967; Mehan and Wood, 1975; Leiter, 1980), tacit knowledge, and the social activities that constitute doing statistics. Ethnostatistics as a domain of empirical inquiry complements statistics as a technical field of science.

Ethnostatistics also complements *enumerology* (Bodgan and Ksander, 1980), the study of how counting actually occurs in organizational settings. Counting or the construction of quantitative data is part of the broader quantitative research process that includes selection and use of particular statistical techniques for manipulating data after counting (development of data, variables, and a database) has occurred. Clearly, then, the field of ethnostatistics is potentially quite broad. Lay generation and uses of numbers or statistics are within this domain (Bogdan and Ksander, 1980), as are the activities and interests of "pure" or "applied" statisticians (MacKenzie, 1978; Norton, 1978). However, given the social science scope and orientation of this methodology series, the emphasis in this monograph is with statistics in the context of professional social science research.

The fundamental concern of ethnostatistics is in describing, analyzing, explaining, and understanding how statistics are actually accomplished and used in the research process. Ethnostatistics thus examines the qualitative aspects of doing statistical analyses, and treats statistical analyses as sources of insight into social processes that underlay scientific knowledge. Interpretive practices and practical knowledge underlay the production and professional uses of statistical facts, and constitute the qualitative bases of quantitative research addressed in this volume.

Examples and Levels of Ethnostatistics

This section describes three examples of ethnostatistics drawn from Garfinkel's (1967) research concerning the process by which psychiatric institutions select patients. The section then outlines three general areas or levels at which ethnostatistics has gone to work.

In the first example, Garfinkel and Bittner undertook field research to investigate criteria used to select potential patients for treatment at the Outpatient Psychiatric Clinic at the UCLA Medical Center (Garfinkel, 1967, chap. 6). The sources of information for the study were (1) the quantitative and qualitative data produced in normally occurring clinic case folders, including intake forms, (2) a special "Clinic Career Form" designed by the investigators and inserted into each case file, and (3) insights gained by direct observation of clinic activities and personnel. The researchers expected the clinic personnel would complete the forms, but found instead that personnel failed to provide information on most items (p. 187). Improved training of research assistants and clinic personnel did not seem to improve the quality of data collected.

Garfinkel and Bittner thus transformed the common problem of missing data into a topic for a qualitative study. First, they created a table that summarized each type of information sought, and the percentage of cases in the study for which the information was available. For example, the table revealed that patients' sex was obtained in 99.8% of cases, but occupation was obtained in only 44.4% of cases. Next, the researchers used the knowledge they gained through field observations to adopt the perspective of clinic personnel. This provided a way of explicating the social features and work interests that account for the variations in data availability that any investigator would encounter. The sources of these "normal, natural troubles" include, for example, the time and effort it takes to collect certain information, and a distaste for paperwork. Thus the practical ease of collecting information appears associated with the information collected. Further, omissions and duplications of information suggest that records reflect producers' anticipations of future but as yet unknown organizational uses of the records. For example, names of intake therapists were recorded in 96.2% of cases, but no information was available for such things as administration of psychological tests, type of recommended treatment, planned visit regime, or number of prior admissions. Future users of such records would be able to determine that therapists were involved in intake work. But since the actual treatment work was not completely described in the case folders, the treatment itself could not be criticized in the future. Therapists could not be held responsible for failing to properly treat experienced "psychos" who later ran amok.

The example illustrates that missing data arise because organizational personnel have established certain "right" ways of reporting their activities, ways that preserve and protect their personal, occupational, and organizational interests (Garfinkel, 1967: 191). Direct observations of data producers and production contexts, as well as knowledge of the cultural worlds of data producers, are necessary to discover and understand the meaning of the data produced. Social scientific uses of quantitative data must explicitly take the context of production into account, and must reconcile the demands of research with the social organizational features embedded in the data.

A second example of ethnostatistics is Garfinkel's attempt to replicate the statistical analyses done in previous selection studies. In attempting to apply statistical rules in a strict manner, he discovered a multitude of points where no clearly correct answers or procedures were available. For example, in undertaking a chi-square analysis, Garfinkel found it necessary to partition a large frequency distribution table into a set of smaller subtables, using Mosteller's explication of Kimball's method of partitioning tables (pp. 258-259). Computing the chi-square required the allocation of degrees of freedom to the subtables, and there were several statistically adequate ways to allocate degrees of freedom. Garfinkel then contacted Professor Mosteller to determine the most appropriate way to partition degrees of freedom. He learned there are no proofs that the different ways of allocating the degrees of freedom will produce identical results. Thus the decision concerning how to allocate degrees of freedom required selection from diverse alternatives. Any selection must be based on practical grounds, and different practical decisions can produce different statistical models, results, and findings.

A third example of ethnostatistics is Garfinkel's (1967) comparative analysis of the contents of published studies of patient selection. The studies claimed to address patient selection by using similar methods, and to produce results and findings that could be compared to those of other studies. But Garfinkel found that different studies handled the various methodological parameters (e.g., comparison populations) differently, and each study failed to handle at least one parameter. Many of the assumptions and methodological decisions that were apparently made were not mentioned in the studies. And the findings of the studies could only be verified by making a large set of assumptions about the very selection criteria that were presumably being measured. Thus statistics were displayed in each selection study so as to persuade the reader that the conclusions of the study were valid. But the methods used to produce the statistics were inadequate to ensure the validity, replicability, and comparability of the statistical results and findings.

The Garfinkel examples illustrate the three levels at which ethnostatistical studies have been conducted. First-order ethnostatistical studies are concerned with producing a statistic. These studies involve detailed, situationally specific ethnographies and qualitative research on the occupational practices of statistics producers at work. These are studies of the cultural features of select occupations, quantitative groups, and scientific tribes or sects, with scientists as the subjects of inquiry. First-order research thus investigates the activities, meanings, and contexts involved in producing variables and statistics. Ethnographies of statistics production require direct empirical observation of the actual behaviors and natural practices of statistics producers, in the everyday life research settings in which they produce use statistics (Gubrium and Buckholdt, 1979).

Second-order ethnostatistics addresses statistics at work. These studies use simulations and statistical methods to explicitly test tacit technical and practical assumptions involved in producing statistics (Labovitz, 1967, 1970; Lieberson, 1985; Gephart, 1983). Technical inquiry is inherent to science (Lynch, 1985a, 1985b) and critical analyses of technical properties of statistics are frequent concerns for quantitative social researchers themselves, independent of particular ethnostatistical interests. Thus many conventional methodological studies address issues of interest to ethnostatistics. The distinctive feature of second-order ethnostatistical studies is the inclusion of social and practical assumptions and features of research in tests of the adequacy of technical alternatives. That is, second-level ethnostatistical studies apply quantitative methods to assess how the researcher, subject, measurement instrument, or the social context of measurement effects measurement outcomes and statistical results and findings (Churchill, 1971).

Third-order ethnostatistical studies treat statistics as rhetoric. They examine scientific reports (texts) that display statistics, treat the reports as events in and of themselves, and analyze the reports as literary accomplishments that use statistics to persuade the reader (Gusfield, 1981; Knorr-Cetina, 1981; McCloskey, 1985; Gephart, 1986). The texts are deconstructed (Harari, 1979; Culler, 1982; Gephart, 1986) by using methods of literary criticism to explicate the underlying literary practices that accomplish the meanings evident in the texts. Third-order ethnostatistical studies provide critiques of the philosophical and epistemological problems involved in using quantitative methods. They also provide insights into how statistics are displayed in the public domain, and how the technical selections and literary practices of researchers provide reified quantitative facts.

Thus the current manuscript provides a general overview of the field of ethnostatistics, but it is not intended as a complete review of the literature in the field. Instead, the primary concern of the volume is with how to conduct ethnostatistical studies of social research at the three levels of analysis: producing statistics, statistics at work, and statistics as rhetoric. Each of the three levels is the subject matter of a subsequent chapter. In each chapter, reasons for the respective type of ethnostatistics are presented, along with examples of research, and discussions of how the research can be conducted. The final chapter discusses the future of ethnostatistics and suggests ways ethnostatistics can be used to improve social research.

2. PRODUCING A STATISTIC

If you want to understand what a science is, you should look in the first
instance not at its theories or its findings, and certainly not at what its
apologists say about it; you should look at what the practitioners of it do
[Geertz, 1973: 5].

Producing a statistic is a social enterprise spanning a range of
activities: A database must be assembled, and this involves selecting
phenomena to measure, making observations and measurements, and
coding results. Variables and statistics must be selected, and the
statistical analysis must be run to produce results and findings. These
activities occur in specific everyday life social settings where practical
constraints and concerns arise to influence the research. Statistics,
following Gusfield (1981: 132), are seen to exist sociologically in the
day-to-day behavior of researchers, statisticians, educational testers,
social scientists, management consultants, and others who produce and
use statistics. The production of statistics occurs in the classroom,
lunchroom, office, lab, and wherever professionals use the rules of
statistics and quantitative methods, and act with reference to them. At
the everyday level, statistics lack the consistency and finality found in
published scientific products (Gusfield, 1981: 167). Their meaning is
negotiable, and is influenced by the relative power of the scientist and
organizational needs. To understand adequately the meaning of statistics as scientific resources and products, one must directly observe
and analyze their construction in specific situations.
   Producing a statistic is often a "tiered situational occurrence"
(Bogdan and Ksander, 1980: 305) and transsituational event that must
be tracked across many different levels of participants and settings. That
is, producing a statistic spans the boundaries of different organizations
and settings. Those who collect data may be different from those who
apply higher-order statistical procedures to the data, and may have
different interests or concerns (Bodgan and Ksander, 1980). Further, the
production and use of statistics in everyday scientific and bureaucratic
settings involves visible rituals in which a conception of social order is
reestablished in agreed upon, shared visions of scientific facts. Statistics
construct an orderly world represented by abstract rules (Gusfield, 1981:
167).

Ethnography and
the Cultures of Science

Ethnography is the use of direct observation and extended field research to produce a thick, naturalistic description of a people and their culture. Ethnography seeks to uncover the symbols and categories members of the given culture use to interpret their world, and ethnography thus preserves the integrity and inherent properties of cultural phenomena (Geertz, 1973; Knorr-Cetina, 1983). Ethnographic methods for naturalistic, anthropological field research have been used to investigate the production of hard data (Kitsuse and Cicourel, 1963; Cicourel, 1974; MacKay, 1974; Roth, 1974; Gubrium and Buckholdt, 1979; Jacobs, 1979). And recent ethnographic studies of natural scientists at work in laboratory settings (Woolgar, 1982; Knorr-Cetina, 1983) have provided rigorous and precise descriptions of the activities and reasoning of natural scientists (e.g., Latour and Woolgar, 1979, 1986; Knorr-Cetina, 1981; Lynch, 1985b). The results of these studies vary with their theoretical concerns. In general, the studies have investigated the indexical and contextually contingent properties of scientific reasoning and facts, and have demonstrated how scientific inquiry can be understood as a process of construction, rather than depiction (Knorr-Cetina, 1983). While the "laboratory studies of science" do not specifically address social scientists, or the production of statistics per se, they emphasize both the technical, methodological practices of natural science, and the practical and social contexts of scientific methods. Thus they serve as excellent models for the kinds of first order ethnostatistical studies that may be undertaken in social science.

Ethnographies of laboratory science seek to provide accounts based on the experience of close daily contacts with scientists in their natural habitats (Latour and Woolgar, 1986: 18). This involves in situ monitoring of scientists' activities in a particular setting, particularly the routine minutiae of daily life (Latour and Woolgar, 1986: 27). They focus on describing the internal affairs of science that are taken to be constructive (Knorr-Cetina, 1981: 4). The laboratory situation is treated as a reality *sui generis*; that is, a reality in its own right that entails constraints, organization, and dynamics that cannot be predicted from the characteristics of individual participants, or from a priori social attributes (Knorr-Cetina, 1981: 43).

Successful ethnographies of science require (1) close examination of the technical culture and (2) the active cooperation of scientists (Latour and Woolgar, 1986: 26). Data are collected through direct observation, interviews, and the accumulation of documents generated by the scientific group under study (Latour and Woolgar, 1986; Knorr-Cetina, 1981; Lynch, 1982, 1985a, 1985b).

The purpose of this chapter is to demonstrate how qualitative, ethnographic methods have been applied in studies of data production and scientific activity, and how one might in the future undertake studies that focus more explicitly on the production of statistics in social science. Features that are unique or specific to ethnographies of statistics production are thus emphasized. The intent here is not to review techniques for how to do field research, ethnography, or social studies of science. The reader is referred to a number of good general texts that address ethnographic and field research methods (McCall and Simmons, 1967; Emerson, 1983; Hammersley and Atkinson, 1983; Speier, 1973; Agar, 1986). Important examples of qualitative, social studies scientific methods can be found in the works of Kuhn (1962), Bittner (1973), Elliot (1974), Bowden (1985), Bijker et al. (1987), Garfinkel et al. (1981), Knorr-Cetina (1981, 1983), Lynch (1982, 1985a, 1985b), Lynch et al. (1983), Latour and Woolgar (1979, 1986), Latour (1987), Mulkay (1984), Mulkay and Gilbert (1983), Woolgar (1980, 1981), and Yeareley (1981). And useful examples of ethnographic research on areas other than science can be found in Cavan (1966), Emerson (1969, 1981), Gephart (1978), Goffman (1959, 1961), Mehan (1979), Sudnow (1967), Silverman (1981), Van Maanen (1973, 1978, 1982, forthcoming), and Kunda (1986).

The remainder of the chapter discusses a total of six examples from three areas where ethnographic methods have been applied to issues germane to ethnostatistics: the production of hard data in social service organizations, the production of measures of intelligence, and the production of scientific knowledge in laboratories. The discussion thus illustrates how ethnographic research can penetrate the quantitative cultures of hard data producers and users and thus bring us into touch with the lives of these interesting strangers (Geertz, 1973: 21).

Area 1: Studying Hard Data Production in Service Organizations

The collection and coding of data involves measurement—the transformation of observations into numbers. Qualitative and ethnographic studies of measurement (see Cicourel, 1964, 1974; Cicourel et al., 1973; Jacobs, 1979; Gubrium and Buckholdt, 1979) have examined the organizational generation of data because many social science data are secondary in nature; that is, data generated through normal bureaucratic processes are used for scientific research purposes. Even the academic collection and production of hard data occurs in organizational settings, and thus the production of quantitative data in service organizations provides insights into the selective collection and coding processes that characterize social science.

As an example, Gubrium and Buckholdt (1979) provide a classic ethnographic analysis of the production and meaning of "hard" data in two social service institutions: a nursing home and a home for emotionally disturbed children. The goal of the study was to contrast "the formal image of hard data held and used by service providers and regulatory agents with the practice of hard data production" (p. 116). The study involved observational fieldwork of professionals from each institution (e.g., nurses, social workers, psychologists, psychiatrists) over several months, during which time the subjects were "accompanied, observed, and/or assisted in their various functions" (p. 117). In particular, the researchers sought to observe and record staff activities during which "frequencies, percentages, and averages" are constructed or interpreted. They determined that hard data were produced in three ways in the institutions: (1) Staff directly observed and counted behaviors of interest, (2) information already available for other purposes was reassessed for new reasons, and (3) staff surveyed individuals who were assumed to know about some behavior and who could report this information.

The researchers therefore sought access to situations where hard data would routinely be produced. They observed staff-patient interactions wherein measures of the effectiveness of organizational programs were produced. They also inspected patient charts in which information is routinely recorded, and they observed staff meetings where "hard data" were discussed and used in decision making. Field notes, including transcripts of interactions, were prepared.

One nice example of the implications of this approach is the finding that not every act that is countable gets counted; acts must be seen as motivated to be counted. For example, a "highly touted bowel training program" (Gubrium and Buckholdt, 1979: 121) was being monitored by staff by counting the number of "clean days" for each patient. On one occasion a researcher observed that Helen, a patient, had fully soiled her bed. This was not recorded as a "dirty day"; the aide reasoned aloud that the patient was learning to control her bowels, but in this case she became angry and "shit everywhere because I was busy helping Stella (another patient) down the hall and you know how she hates Stella" (p. 121). The next day, the aide entered Helen's room, saw her "redfaced and squirming" (p. 122), and then quickly helped Helen to the toilet. Later, the aide informed the charge nurse that Helen was clean all day, thereby recording a "clean day" for Helen.

Gubrium and Buckholdt determined that, for institution staff, "hard data are believed to mirror the 'real stuff' of behavior better than any other form of description" (p. 119). "This image reflects a view of descriptive rigor present in modern society at large"(p. 119), a view that accords a factual status to quantitative data that seems denied to qualitative data. And yet, by identifying the circumstantial rules and glossing practices by which hard data are produced, they are able to conclude that "the imprecision and lack of concreteness present in hard data are at least equal to that present in any other form of data"(p. 135).

Area 2: Studying the Production of Intelligence Measures

A second area that has been investigated in ethnographic studies of ethnostatistics is intelligence testing. Intelligence testing is designed to produce hard measures of intellectual ability; it has also produced a long history of intellectual disputes including controversy regarding the racial basis of intelligence (Gould, 1981). Since intelligence tests are widely used to select students for educational tracks (Cicourel and Kitsuse, 1963), investigation of intelligence testing will provide insights into how important measures and statistics are produced. This section discusses two specific studies of the measurement of intelligence (MacKay, 1974; Roth, 1974) that emerged as part of a research program concerning student performance in schools (Cicourel et al., 1973).

Cicourel et al. (1973) used the research strategy of indefinite triangulation to study school performance, including the measurement of intelligence, in two school districts in Southern California. Indefinite triangulation involves providing details of different interpretations of the same event by different actors. It allows one to determine how "different physical, temporal, and biographically provided perspectives on a situation" (Cicourel et al., 1973: 4) affect interpretations. The strategy provides a qualitative, ethnographic approach to understanding the "environmental" influences on intelligence.

First, researchers determined the different kinds of information they expected to be available in classroom lessons. Next, the lessons were observed and videotaped. Third, the children and the teachers were interviewed and interrogated about the lesson. Fourth, the teacher was asked to reconstruct the lesson, its purposes, and goals. Fifth, the teacher was shown a videotape of the lesson, and asked to again describe the lesson. The different interpretations were then compared to observations recorded on video or audio tape, and to direct observations of the researcher. This maximized the number of ways in which activity could be examined.

Example 1. Roth (1974) applied indefinite triangulation to standardized tests of students' abilities, in an effort to determine the role of background knowledge and social context in intelligence test performance. The Peabody Picture Vocabulary Test was administered to a sample of black and white school children, both at home and at school, and the testing sessions were tape recorded. To improve data quality, recorders were turned on for as much of the session as possible, and the testers themselves transcribed the tapes "in order to maximize the ability of the transcriber to identify events in the tapes by memory of the testing session" (Roth, 1974: 160).

Roth (1974) used an expansion model (Cicourel, 1980: 111-118) for sociolinguistic analysis of his transcripts. Transcripts were reviewed on a line-by-line basis, and a written commentary was prepared describing key concepts exemplified by the data, as well as the background knowledge necessary to understand what the participants intended and how the interaction was proceeding (Cicourel, 1980: 112). Roth presents the analysis in a table with two adjacent columns, one containing numbered segments of transcripts of interaction during testing and a second containing the researcher's expansion or interpretive analysis of the transcript segment. For example, adjacent to a segment where a tester asks the subject to "tell me what's its name," an interpretation is given that the subject thinks he or she is being asked for "the proper name of picture 1." The expansion analysis allows researchers to remain close to the substantive details of specific interactions, and to demonstrate to the reader of the analysis how analytical conclusions were reached. The reader can inspect the description and adjacent analysis, and assess for oneself the sensibility and face validity of conclusions offered by the researchers. In any given study, the entire set of transcript data should be exhaustively analyzed in this way, although published papers typically report only key segments of the analysis due to page constraints. (For other examples of expansion analysis of transcripts, see, e.g., Turner, 1972; Gephart, 1978, 1979; Mehan, 1979.)

Roth's strategy is to show the subject is able to display intellectual skills assessed by the test, but that responses to test items are counted as incorrect because of features of the local environment, the test stimuli, the rules of testing, or the interpretations of the tester. Conventional testing theory presumes that test administration is a standard procedure. But Roth (1974: 215) shows that standardized procedures cannot be maintained and "are not effective in probing children's background knowledge" because the subject and the tester have to adapt to one another's actions. For example, the presentation of each item to the subject was accompanied by a conversation that was significantly more complex than the simple question-answer response pair that such tests presuppose. An item that asked the child to select a picture of a scholar from several pictures led to a lengthy discussion in which the child made five different types of choices, four of which were not serious. For example, the child picked a picture before being told the type of actor to select. This was clearly an incorrect answer, but it revealed the child's use of complex reasoning practices to transform the interaction into a game whereby he asked questions of the tester: "I bet you don't know the man who is carrying something," remarked the child, as the investigator probed for yet another "sensible" response.

Example 2. Another example is a study by MacKay (1974) that sought to determine if intelligence tests measure the skills they purport to measure. MacKay contrasted correct answers designated by test constructors with the reasons students gave for their answers. In one item, the child is presented with a stimulus, "I went for a ride," and is asked to select from three pictures; a boy swimming, a boy walking, and an auto (p. 232). The officially correct answer is the car, but this assumes only one interpretation of the item is correct; riding refers to cars. As an alternative, MacKay notes that the verb "went" suggests the ride has ended. If the child assumes that the correct answer refers to what is being done now, or after the ride, then pictures of the boy walking or riding could be correct, since the pictures depict current activity to which the stimulus seems to refer; I went for a ride to the pool, so now I am swimming (or walking). Thus MacKay demonstrates that tests fail "because of ambiguity in many items" (p. 245). The ambiguity or indexicality of items is resolved by presuming the constructor's commonsense view of correct answers is absolutely correct and the constructor's view becomes an objective measure of performance.

Area 3: Studying the Production of Science in Laboratories

The production of scientific knowledge in laboratories is a third area where the kinds of ethnographic research necessary in ethnostatistics have been undertaken. In this section, I present a discussion of three "laboratory studies of science" (Knorr-Cetina, 1983) that have used ethnographic methods in distinct ways.

Example 1. The first published "laboratory" study of science to emerge was Latour and Woolgar's (1979; 1986) study of scientists at the Salk Institute. Their distinct perspective was the use of ethnography as a form of anthropological estrangement. The concern was to use an anthropological approach to construct an account of scientific work, based on directly observing scientists in situ. The anthropological perspective, as defined by Latour and Woolgar (1979: 27-30), requires an observer to work hard to retain an outsider's estranged view of the laboratory, and to avoid going native. This is similar to having an anthropologist live with a savage tribe in an exotic locale, and then return from the exotic land to write a report on life among the natives. Participant observation is done in a particular naturally occurring setting to allow one to go beyond scientists' own descriptions of their behavior, and thereby to see the craft nature of science.

The observer assumes the posture of anthropological strangeness by bracketing experience to ensure that taken-for-granted aspects of the lab appear strange. This dissolves, not affirms, the exotic nature of the scientific culture under study. To ensure success, it is necessary to *deny* that one must acquire the superior technological knowledge held by tribespeople if one is to understand their behavior. Estrangement depicts laboratory activities "as those of a remote culture" and allows one to "explore the way in which an ordered account of the laboratory life can be generated without recourse to the explanatory concepts of the inhabitants themselves" (Latour and Woolgar, 1986: 39-40).

This stance is difficult to sustain because one already has a body of commonsense knowledge about laboratories that can be used to interpret and make sensible the activities observed therein (Latour and Woolgar, 1979: 44). Yet one must avoid going native because doing so can result in an account of the scientific tribe in its own terms; such an account is incomprehensible and unhelpful to nonmembers (pp. 38-39) and involves a loss of analytical distance (p. 275). To protect against going native, participants' uses of concepts are treated as empirical topics that require explanation, rather than as resources with obvious meaning. This is facilitated if one avoids strict application of the dramaturgical metaphor and seeks instead to produce a description that forces the reader of the ethnography to take the role of the observer, by presenting data that are not preinterpreted.

The observer in this study was Latour, who had some anthropological training, limited command of the English language, and a general ignorance of science (Latour and Woolgar, 1986: 30). The laboratory was chosen because a senior researcher there provided access to the lab, documents, and personnel, as well as part-time employment to Latour as a lab technician. The researcher later received a Nobel Prize for the work investigated by Latour and Woolgar, thus suggesting the setting was also an important one. Some 21 months of participant observation yielded a large volume of data: (1) voluminous field notes; (2) literature by lab members, including all the research reports by lab members; (3) a wide range of other documents, including letters, data sheets, and drafts of articles; (4) formal interviews of members of the lab and members of other labs; and (5) reflections of the observer, particularly in relation to his work as a lab technician (p. 39). Office space was provided to the observer in the lab, and the observer presented several seminars concerning the research. Thus the research role was overt and reasonably high profile.

This approach is useful where the composition of a society or culture is uncertain or unknown to the researcher. The key advantages of this ethnography from the outside are that it allows the researcher the freedom to define the nature of the setting, to see problems in sense making, to reveal taken-for-granted cultural assumptions of the group under study (Latour and Woolgar, 1986: 278-279), and thus to produce a description of scientific work "relatively unhindered by retrospective reconstruction" (p. 282).

By carefully recording conversations and activities, the researcher can "focus on the routine exchanges and gestures that pass between scientists and on the way in which such minutiae are seen to give rise to logical arguments, the implementation of proofs, and the operation of so called thought processes" (Latour and Woolgar, 1979: 151). In the current study, Latour and Woolgar were able to observe directly how the accepted factual status of statements fluctuated, and this allowed them to describe stages in the emergence of scientific facts "as if a laboratory was a factory where facts were produced on an assembly line" (p. 236).

Example 2. A second distinctive ethnographic approach to the study scientific activities and reasoning practices is use of a sensitive methodology—one that gets us close enough to phenomena to glimpse its true character (Knorr-Cetina, 1981). This requires engagement rather than detachment, involving "direct, unmediated, and prolonged confrontation" (p. 17) with the situation. This leads one to observe how intersubjectivity is a problem for members as well as the researcher, because it "forces us to dismiss the methodological intermediaries generally used for collecting data" (p. 23). The researcher enters the field him- or herself to engage in direct observation and participation.

Knorr-Cetina's observations focused on the content of scientists' practical reasoning in plant protein research in a potato protein laboratory at Berkeley, and did not focus on a group of individuals per se. Thus the specific observational group was constantly changing, and varied in size and administrative composition. To get at the meanings of scientists, the researcher had to rely for data on scientists' talk, scientific documents, and the sequential drafts of scientific papers. This provided exposure "to the savage meaning of the scientist's laboratory action" (p. 23). For example, lengthy involvement in the field and the development of the trust of subjects enabled Knorr-Cetina (p. 45) to observe the deceitful practices a scientist used to gain access to a particular piece of equipment controlled by another researcher.

A sensitive methodology also requires the researcher to let the situation speak for itself. Descriptions that emerge must conserve meaning by remaining faithful to the field of observation (Knorr-Cetina, 1981: 26). This is difficult, but it can be accomplished in part by using tape and video recordings to allow for rigorous microprocess analysis (p. 18). One can also decenter constructivity by letting the field of study exert its own constraints on information (p. 19). For example, by using field notes, interview data, and the series of actual drafts produced by scientists as data to be analyzed, Knorr-Cetina let the naturally occurring data and unwritten meanings of the scientist drive her description and analysis of the scientist as a literary reasoner. And the ethnographer must remain interested in the practices of scientists, and not their cognitions. Thus units of observation must be constructed to allow for the temporal, contextual, and interactional features of action to emerge (p. 19), and interaction, not individual behavior, must be treated as the source of contextual and temporal features of action.

There are several problems in applying sensitive methods to scientific labs (Knorr-Cetina, 1981). The social scientist is an intruder, and the natural scientist has resources to ward off encroachment, in contrast, for example, to prisoners or mental patients. Further, the scientist has little time to answer researchers' questions, given the pressures for publications (Knorr-Cetina, 1981: 24). The social scientist might become an embarrassment and in any event will be a "pain in the neck" when shadowing scientists about. And the social scientist, forced into cramped laboratory quarters alongside the subjects of study, faces a different social situation than the anthropologist camping in a tent near the village of natives. These problems are likely to be all the more salient and significant in ethnostatistical research, when the subjects become our colleagues and ourselves.

Example 3. A third distinct perspective for ethnographic studies of natural science laboratories is provided by Lynch (1982, 1985a, 1985b), who undertook extensive field research in a brain science laboratory at the University of California, Irvine. Lynch (1985b) emphasizes the importance of having the researcher attempt to go native by acquiring a native competence in the technical skills, knowledge, and tasks inherent to the setting. Any ethnographic study of scientific work practices "must, first of all, contend with what scientific practitioners produce and recognize as a competent interpretation, evaluation, or argument in their local setting of inquiry" (Lynch, 1985a: 511). Thus Lynch (1985b) acquired the neurological knowledge and skills necessary to perform routine laboratory tasks, and to talk sensibly with researchers in the laboratories.

Lynch prepared field notes as well as detailed transcripts of tape-recorded, naturally occurring laboratory shop talk. The focus was on mundane moments in the history of the lab's research (Lynch, 1985a: 513), and the "innumerable occasions of collaborative exchange occurring in the day-to-day work of lab members" (1985a: 513). For example, Lynch (1982) sought to address the role of "critical inquiry" in brain science research by determining what critical inquiry looks like as an endogenous feature of laboratory science. Critical inquiry involves practices used to criticize the technical features and adequacy of methods and facts. Conventionally, critical inquiry is conceived in terms of "various academic investigations of the 'hidden motives' and 'forgotten origins' of technical labor in science" (Lynch, 1982: 510). That is, critical inquiry is designed to discover and rectify the technical problems and limits of research that have emerged as a result of sociohistorical contingencies that are not specified in the research itself. In contrast, Lynch (1982) treats critical inquiry as "a significant feature of scientific activity to be investigated in specific disciplinary setting where it arises as a constituent practice" (p. 501).

The endogenous nature of critical inquiry as a concern of scientists while doing research is substantiated in a transcript of a brief conversation between the lab director and a graduate student concerning an electron micrographic montage that documents axon sprouting in the brain tissue of a rat (Lynch, 1982). The transcript fragment is treated as representative of the larger "whole" of mundane laboratory activities and Lynch provides an example of such a montage in his paper. An expansion analysis of the transcript is used (Lynch, 1982: 515-516) to show how the montage documents the inherent nature of critical inquiry in lab work. The analysis proceeds by examining the transcript line by line and "specifying how the locutions on the transcript thematized, and worked with, the details of the montage record" (p. 515). For example, the lab director and the assistant discuss the ambiguity of the montage, and the role of the research assistant in producing a problematic depiction: "Shot that a little high, didn't yeh?" (p. 514, line 10). The assistant responds in the negative, but the transcript is an incomplete guide to the meaning of actors' statements. For example, the assistant states "no, but I mean it . . . it's really densely . . . I don't know if it's sprouting er'r normal population right in here" (p. 514, lines 17-19). Lynch's expansion elaborates the meaning of the statements: The assistant defends his prior practices by implying there were no easy technical solutions that would ensure that the area of interest was contained in the montage, because the photos show the ambiguous character of the axons.

The task of the expansion analysis is "one of using the visibility of the montage display to explicate matters of social relevance, that is, matters of practical responsibility, competence, and fortune" (p. 518). To do this, one must make explicit the tacit background knowledge, and particularly technical issues and options, which make the conversation sensible to the participants and to the reader. This requires the researcher to possess, utilize, and surface considerable technical knowledge, as well as knowledge of the history, features, and ethnographic particulars of the laboratory and the research undertaken.

Prospects for Future Research

First-level ethnostatistical studies use qualitative and ethnographic methods to study the naturally occurring activities, settings, and meanings of social scientists (and others) involved in producing statistics. While there are examples of ethnographic research concerning how "hard" social data are constructed (Gubrium and Buckholdt, 1979; Roth, 1974: MacKay, 1974), the actual process of using statistical procedures after data are available (doing statistical analysis) has not been extensively explored with ethnographic methods. Statistics texts (e.g., Kerlinger and Pedhazur, 1973) describe ideal procedural routines, technical criteria, and mathematical formulae. Critical assessments of methods have addressed the social features of measurement, by critiquing published quantitative studies (Garfinkel, 1967; Pawson, 1982) or common practices (Labovitz, 1967; Lieberson, 1985: Guttman, 1977). What is required to complement such works are rigorous and systematic ethnographic studies of social science researchers at work, where the production of a statistic is a central theme, in both the workday activities of scientists, and in the research focus of the study. That is, there is need for discovery-oriented ethnographic studies that describe the practical aspects of technical selections involved in producing statistics, where these aspects are uncovered and evidenced in specific activities and situations. At present, there are relatively few ethnographic studies of the exotic domain of quantitative social researchers.

The practicalities of producing a statistic should become a topic for first-level ethnostatistics. One's native knowledge of the cultural aspects of social science can thus be used to identify practicalities of statistics use, and to gain access to settings in which social scientists produce and use statistics. A number of regularly occurring formal organizational rituals could become potential research settings, for example, academic research symposia wherein researchers describe quantitative studies. These seminars could be audio- or videotaped, and the discussions involving statistical aspects of the research would clearly be germane to ethnostatistics. It would also be of interest to investigate job interview seminars or theses defenses where the candidate is challenged to display significant technical competence in statistics and quantitative methods. A variety of theoretical interests could be served by studies that address the cultures of quantification. For example, norms that encourage and legitimate quantification might be discovered.

Another formal setting is the classroom. Ethnographic studies of teaching social statistics and quantitative methods would illuminate problems students have in acquiring appropriate background knowledge, and in transforming abstract technical knowledge into procedures in use. Similarly, the practices that statistics instructors use to bring closure to potentially vague procedural rules could be uncovered, as could the qualitative and quantitative bases of assessments of statistical competence.

Informal rituals and interactions in the habitat of the quantitative researcher can also be usefully investigated. This habitat includes computer rooms, offices, lunch rooms, and anywhere that producing a statistic "happens." The task would be to follow the natives around to discover their social habits and work activities, and the contexts and settings where the business of statistics arises.

Further, many if not most organizations in contemporary society produce and use statistical information. Studies of the generation of hard data by social service organizations (Gubrium and Buckholdt, 1979) could be complemented by studies of organizations that produce measures or statistics as central products (e.g., polling firms, or a university's center for survey research). Given the importance of such organizations, analyses of their organizational cultures (Schein, 1985) would prove insightful.

The socialization of quantitative researchers could also become a concern in ethnostatistics. For example, the prospects and problems of producing statistics could be clarified by the production of what Van Maanen (forthcoming) calls "tales of the field." These tales are thick descriptions of researcher activities and foibles written by the researchers themselves. Further, it may be possible to identify stages in the socialization process of quantitative researchers, that is, stages of learning statistics. This socialization could be regarded as socialization into a legitimate profession (Van Maanen, 1973), or a deviant occupation (Becker, 1963) where stigmatization occurs (Goffman, 1963), with different consequences likely to emerge from each perspective. And relatively little is known about why or how people select quantitative careers or come to advocate quantitative methods rather than qualitative methods. Finally, this type of research could be used simply to describe what good quantitative researchers do, and how they do it well.

This work would improve understanding of the process of producing a statistic. Activities and issues that lie beyond statistics texts will emerge, as will the reasons and meanings behind technical choices and selections. Such research can thus help demystify quantitative social research by showing its practical bases and limits.

3. STATISTICS AT WORK

These statistics, however accidental and therefore uninstructive they may appear, as they have a certain completeness, have a certain value also [Thoreau, 1854/1985: 53].

This chapter addresses statistics at work, the second level of ethnostatistical studies. Second-level studies investigate the adequacy of basic technical and practical assumptions made in statistical analyses. Two types of taken-for-granted assumptions made in the quantitative research process are of particular interest: (1) technical methodological or statistical assumptions where alternatives are available, and (2) implicit assumptions about the cognitive or social features of the research process. Second-order studies employ quantitative methods and statistical procedures in a technically reflective manner. Researchers seek to explicate and critique potentially problematic assumptions and practices, and to propose more adequate alternatives. This is the domain of quantitative methodologists concerned with practical, social constraints on the validity and utility of statistical results and findings. Examples of these second-level ethnostatistical issues can be found in the works of Labovitz (1967, 1970, 1972), Guttman (1977, 1982), Henkel (1975), Henry (1982), O'Brien (1979, 1981a, 1981b, 1982), Bollen and Barb (1981), Johnson and Creech (1983), Kim (1975), Martin (1975, 1978), Lieberson (1985), Gephart (1983), Maimon et al. (1980, 1986), Pawson (1982), Gould (1981), Cowger (1984), and Winship and Mare (1984).

Second-level ethnostatistical studies take the perspective of the user of quantitative methods and statistical procedures, to discover and assess the limits of particular quantitative/statistical practices. Many social contextual features of concern in first-level studies are glossed over and/or accepted as nonproblematic in second-level studies. The task in putting statistics to work is to identify and test a limited set of technical and practical features of interest, rather than to describe the entire complex of social constraints.

The rationale for second-level ethnostatistics is that methodological assumptions "should be thoroughly scrutinized by the researcher before selecting a statistical technique" (Labovitz, 1967: 160). These assumptions are seldom tested, and if they are inappropriate or incorrect, then social measurement is problematic. Alternatively, tests may show that "certain assumptions of both descriptive and inference statistics can be violated without unduly altering the conclusions" (Labovitz, 1967: 151), and thus testing may legitimate and validate practices that are avoided or employed only with reservations. Lieberson (1985) is more direct concerning conventional quantitative social science: "Many of the procedures and assumptions in this enterprise are of no more merit than a quest for a perpetual motion machine . . . even worse . . . some of the normal practices in empirical social research are actually counterproductive" (p. ix). Second-level ethnostatistical studies are thus informed by critical studies of quantitative research conducted by advocates of quantification. The general difference between conventional methodological studies and ethnostatistics is that conventional studies are primarily or exclusively concerned with technical and/or statistical parameters of variables and distributions. They lack a direct concern for the social aspects of quantitative analysis and statistics, and the potentially different sense making of researchers and subjects. In contrast, second-level ethnostatistical studies specify and test explicit models of the practical reasoning of researchers and subjects. Social factors involved in measurement and the construction of variables are important testable parameters. Indeed, the general interest is explicating the problematic interface between the social features or requirements of measurement and the technical operations of statistics.

A primary methodological tactic in second-level ethnostatistics is to "make trouble" by identifying the major problems in using a particular procedure or assumption: "Procedurally it is my preference to start with familiar scenes and ask what can be done to make trouble" (Garfinkel, 1967: 37). One proceeds by performing operations that "multiply the senseless features of perceived environments; to produce and sustain bewilderment, consternation, and confusion" (pp. 37-38). Methodologists are encouraged to identify problems, even if no alternatives or solutions seem available, since "nothing is gained by avoiding that which the discipline must face up to sooner or later" (Lieberson, 1985: xiii).

Clearly, there are reasons for leaving assumptions tacit and untested. One may not even be aware one is making the assumptions, or the assumptions may in fact be untestable. The social scientist may lack the technical knowledge and training necessary to fully understand the mathematical background of the statistics, or to formulate elegant and forceful tests of assumptions. Finally, given publish-or-perish pressures, the social scientist may well be more concerned with understanding how to use generally accepted procedures than with challenging or undermining the procedures or their assumptions. Challenging taken-for-granted assumptions of quantitative research may not appeal to researchers, who feel they can ill afford to spend time challenging the establishment. Yet such challenges are important ways of making contributions. Further, established researchers have reputations and careers that are built on use of specific techniques. They thus are less likely to challenge assumptions and propose alternatives because they have a vested interest in preserving the utility of the established techniques, and, further, the taken-for-granted assumptions have become invisible through familiarity (Garfinkel, 1967).

The remainder of this chapter discusses a total of five examples from three important areas or ways in which researchers have put statistics to work to critically assess and make trouble with the assumptions made in applying quantitative methods in social science. The first area assesses the adequacy of quasi-experimental research designs for social research. Two examples are discussed here: the assumed usefulness of control variables, and the assumption that causation is symmetrical. The second area assesses the adequacy of using the parametric strategy to transform data to meet statistical assumptions. Two examples of the second approach are discussed: the initial study in the area (Labovitz, 1970), and a later one concerned with the effects of highly imprecise measures (Gephart, 1983). The third approach assesses the effect of tacit assumptions on causal models. The example discussed here concerns path analysis.

Area 1: Assessing the Experimental Paradigm

Lieberson (1985) is a "native" statistician who recently offered a provocative and self-reflective assessment of statistics at work. He attempts to "reform and mold empirical research into an activity that contributes as much as possible to a rigorous understanding of society" (p. 13). Lieberson is "fully sympathetic with the empirical research goals found in much of contemporary American sociology, with its emphasis on rigor and quantification" (p. ix). His concern is that the natural science experiment is incorrectly treated as a basic analogy for social research, hence social data are incorrectly interpreted as if they were truly generated by controlled experiments.

The true experiment requires random assignment of subjects to treatment conditions; random selection is not generally possible in social science, because selective processes are operative and result in quasi-experimental designs (Lieberson, 1985: 14-15). Lieberson explores the consequences of assuming experimental controls are operative when they are not. In general, he uses logical proofs, and quantitative simulations or demonstrations to substantiate his points. While his book is actually a sophisticated textbook concerning problems with traditional statistical methods, the book provides several good examples of issues in second-level ethnostatistics. Two examples from Lieberson are discussed below to illustrate the approach he takes.

Example 1. First, Lieberson notes that users of the quasi-experimental model assume that experimental controls can be obtained by using control variables to remove the effects of unmeasured selectivity. By unmeasured selectivity, he means nonrandom factors, such as personal choice, that effect the selection of subjects or their assignment to experimental treatments and hence impact on dependent variables. In a true experiment, selectivity is removed or negated by random assignment of subjects to treatments. Lieberson (1985: 21-32) demonstrates how, in cases of unmeasured selectivity, the application of control variables "will only rarely determine what the 'true' relationships would have been, had there been random assignment conditions under an actual experiment" (p. 31). Indeed, "under some conditions, the application of controls generates results that are actually farther removed from the truth than would occur if no controls were applied" (p. 22). Further, none of the selective processes is unique to a specific statistical procedure (p. 32), and the selectivity massively influences observed results (p. 17).

Example 2. A second example concerns the assumption made in most quasi-experimental designs that causation is symmetrical (Lieberson,

1985: 63). That is, X and Y are assumed to covary in both directions; both are assumed to either increase or decrease together, and the effects of the independent variable are assumed to be reversible. Yet asymmetrical causal relations can exist, for instance, where increasing X increases Y, but where, thereafter, decreasing X does not decrease Y, or decreases it in a nonproportionate manner (Lieberson 1985: 65-66). Much social policy research is based on the likely incorrect assumption that causation is symmetric, hence removing the cause removes the effects (p. 72). The implication is that if a cause is not reversible, removing the cause will not improve the situation.

Lieberson (1985) discusses a number of other problems in conventional quantitative social science that are of interest to ethnostatistics. And he proposes a range of useful suggestions for improving quantitative research. The book thus provides several illustrations of the kinds of second-level ethnostatistical studies one could undertake, and the conclusions that might result. The reader may wish to consult Lieberson's work directly for further ideas and examples.

Area 2: Assessing the Adequacy of the Parametric Strategy

The parametric strategy is a means for transforming nominal or ordinal data into interval-level measures (Labovitz, 1967, 1970; Kim, 1975; O'Brien, 1979, 1981a, 1981b, 1982; Hensler and Stipak, 1979; Bollen and Barb, 1981). The parametric strategy assigns interval scale values to nominal or ordinal categories. For example, an ordinal measure is produced if subjects rank order 10 items according to how much they like these (10 = most liked, 9 = next most liked, and so on). The scale involves relative rank order differences in magnitude of liking, and not absolute or equidistant liking values, since the most liked item (which receives a score of 10) is not necessarily liked 10 times as much as the least liked item (score = 1). The parametric strategy assumes one can treat the ordinal scores as representing an underlying continuous variable with equal distance between categories by simply assigning the values (1-10) to the ranks as if they are appropriate interval measures.

The parametric strategy allows one to analyze nominal or ordinal data with parametric statistics. Parametric statistics require interval measurement of variables since the statistics assume a normally distributed population with precisely specified parameters of central tendency (e.g., a mean) and dispersion (e.g., standard deviation). The parametric strategy is thus an important way of avoiding the " 'under-measurement dilemma" that social sciences face (Acock and Martin, 1974) because of the fact that social science instruments typically cannot produce true interval measures (p. 427). The parametric strategy has a long history of use in social science, and this may have limited the use of nonparametric statistics. Thus second-level ethnostatistics has investigated the adequacy of the parametric strategy because of its widespread use and importance to social science.

Example 1. The first example of assessing the adequacy of the parametric strategy is provided by Labovitz (1967, 1970). He set out to demonstrate that the parametric strategy was appropriate in social science. Essentially, he sought to legitimate the taken-for-granted assumption that one could ignore the basic level of measurement assumptions in regression analysis. Labovitz (1967, 1970) ran an experimental computer simulation by computing correlations (rP) on two variables to which a number of different scoring systems had been applied. In the more extensive study (Labovitz, 1970), the two variables were (1) NORC occupational prestige rating for 36 occupations, an ordinal variable with 36 categories, and (2) suicide rate, a ratio variable. For the occupational prestige variable, interval values were randomly assigned to the categories, using 20 different scoring systems (treatments or ways of assigning values). One scoring system was actual ranking given in an actual study, another was a true interval scale with categories of equal size and equidistant values assigned to each category. Some 18 other systems were used to score or assign measured values to the independent variable; these used values randomly selected from a standard distribution. By assuming each scoring system in turn is the "true" measure, a correlation matrix (rP) for the 20 systems indicates the error involved in using the other scoring systems (Labovitz, 1970: 517). In this matrix, all 190 correlations are above .9, and 157 are above .97, hence Labovitz argues that under at least some conditions, imperfect scoring systems (measurement) will have negligible effects on statistical results (p. 520).

Labovitz then compared the correlations (rP) for suicide rates and the 20 scoring systems of occupational prestige. The true rho value (an ordinal measure of association appropriate to actual level of measurement of occupational prestige) was .07, whereas the rP was .11. Correlations for the other scoring systems and suicide rate range between .09 and .15. Labovitz notes, "These results substantiate the point that different systems yield interchangeable variables" (p. 521). The study generally concludes that the parametric strategy does not distort correlation values or their interpretability, hence ordinal variables could be used with rP and, implicitly, multiple R. A number of other researchers have since devised various scoring systems that they then used to determine the limits of utility of the parametric strategy.

Example 2. It is useful to discuss in detail a second example of assessing the parametric strategy with an emphasis on how the study was done. The example is taken from a study I conducted in which the adequacy of using the parametric strategy in multiple regression and path analyses, where data have varying levels of measurement imprecision, was assessed (Gephart, 1983). The study thus tests the taken-for-granted assumption that the parametric strategy is adequate, and that ordinal data can be treated "as if" they are interval data when doing regressions. An interesting feature of the study is an attempt to link measurement imprecision to implicit models of the subject and measurement instruments used.

Conventional methodologies implicitly assume a model of the subject or actor as a rational being capable of assigning quantitative values to qualitative phenomena consistently and reliably using the criteria or meanings desired by the social scientist. Further, it is assumed that response categories are interpreted in the same way by different people, that phenomena being measured have real quantitative underlying dimensions that correspond directly to measurement scales, and that the subjects can report true values (Cicourel, 1964; Pawson, 1982). These assumptions reflect practical, social features of measurement, not statistical criteria or technical rules. And the assumptions may not be valid. Further, Lieberson (1985) suggests that where implicit models of actors are inadequate and measurement of variables is imprecise, quantitative methods may produce unrecognized distortions of true measures and statistics.

An alternative nonrational model of the social actor assumes the actor lacks complete information, behaves inconsistently, and has difficulty assigning numbers to experiences. If assignment of numbers is somewhat arbitrary, different actors understand things differently and hence different subjects have different meanings for the same values and variables. One can still assume that there are true interval values for variables, but that actors have difficulties in reporting these values, or that measurement instruments have trouble in capturing these values.

With the implicit nonrational model of the actor or measure, the best that social science can do is to produce roughly ordinal measures. Thus some subjects will respond with values of, for example, 4 where other subjects have the same meaning, but respond with 5. Similarly, subjects forget previous selections and give a 5 one time and a 4 the next time. Some subjects will use a wide range of values and others will report restricted ranges of values. Many or most subjects can rank things only vaguely; the value 2 has no absolute meaning. And some subjects have wide intervals where others have narrow ones, for example, good to one subject might be 90 on a 100-point scale, whereas good to another is 2 on a 3-point scale.

To test the effects of the different implicit models, an experiment was undertaken by varying the levels of measurement imprecision and assessing the effects on parametric statistics. Here, measurement precision varied from minimally ordinal measures to a situation where true interval values were precisely, reliably, and validly obtained. The null hypothesis was that imprecise measurement will produce statistics (multiple Rs and beta values) equivalent to true values. The alternative hypothesis was that observed values will differ from true values, since there will be distortion induced by any measurement imprecision. Further, it was expected that unequal interval scaling will produce greater distortion of statistics than measurement using equal interval scales, and that the greater the number of categories the less the distortion.

The database for the experiment was a secondary data file of 1970 census data composed of 50 ratio-level sociodemographic variables with measures for each of the 50 states in the United States, hence the sample size was 50. Four variables were selected from the database for purposes of analysis: (1) murder rate, (2) percentage nonwhite in the population, (3) divorce rate, and (4) rate of high school dropouts. Criteria for selecting the variables were that (1) the underlying distributions of the variables met all the assumptions of multiple R, and (2) the variables were suitable for path analysis and formed a system linked by fewer than the (six) maximum paths possible.

The experiment required a method for producing defective measures so that the statistical results that emerge from defective measures could be compared to "true" values. A total of five scales were used. The original ratio data were treated as true values of the variables, and then two of the four independent variables (percentage nonwhite, and divorce rate) were imperfectly remeasured using the four transformations discussed below. First, two interval scoring systems were constructed. These preserve the interval measurement of the variable, but collapse a range of values into a more restricted range. Thus information is lost, and some distortion occurs. The first interval rescaling involved four equal intervals, where variables were assigned the values of 1 to 4, consistent with the ordered pattern of true values. Here, a range of different true values are grouped into equal-size intervals. For example, percentage nonwhite ranged from 0 to 60, so the values from 0 to <15 were all assigned the new interval value of 1; interval 2 was 15 to < 30, and so forth. This scale represents a situation where there is consistency across actors (or instruments) in terms of responses to the proper interval, but true values have wider ranges (0 to 60, with 60 intervals, and continuous ratio values available) than actors can report or than instruments can capture, since only 4 intervals with a range of 1 to 4 are now available. Hence different absolute values are bunched together in the same interval. The measurement scale is thus reliable and accurate, but can't use all the information that is potentially available. The second equal interval system used 12 equal intervals that were constructed as above. Here, the range of 60 values is compressed, but the compression into 12 intervals is less severe than with 4 intervals, so more information is used. This is the most precise scale of measurement used, after the true values.

Next, two even "worse" instruments were constructed. The first involved four unequal intervals constructed by starting at 0, then selecting three 3-digit random numbers (within the range of true values) from a random numbers table, as break points for intervals. The largest observed true value was used as the top end of the range for the highest scored interval. For example, divorce rate ranged as high as 6%; the first randomly selected interval was 0 to < .6, the second was .6 to < 2.6, the third interval was 2.6 to < 3.9 and the final interval was 3.9 to 6. Monotonically increasing values were assigned to increasing intervals. Here, actors and measures are their least precise, and can at best capture rather vague ordinal values. However, a range of very different values may get bunched together into the same category, and the categories represent or reflect pure, limited ranking and say little about the underlying values. The final defective scoring system (measure) used 12 unequal intervals and was constructed by randomly determining interval widths and assigning values of 1 to 12 to the intervals, in increasing order. Here, actors can clearly rank things, though inconsistently, and the absolute underlying values remain hidden. Different values will be bunched together. Actors still can't report all they know, or measurement instruments cannot capture all the information.

After the data were rescored, bivariate regressions were run for all combinations of the variables and treatment conditions. This produced a correlation matrix, which is presented below in Table 3.1.

The results are interesting. The equal intervals scales provide a good test of the adequacy of the parametric strategy in which one can assume that measurement can be fairly precise, and that actors carry true interval values in their heads, are consistent across time and among one another, and are given response options that reflect their values. With the greatest precision (12 equal intervals) one finds little distortion; observed values correlate highly with true values, for example r = .99176 for NONWH and .98296 for divorce. Although values drop where only four intervals are used, in some cases the drop is small (e.g., NONWH drops from .98296 to .93502), in others it is larger, although a sizable correlation remains. When the number of imprecisely measured variables is increased, the correlation of true to observed values drops but the values are not widely discrepant from true values.

The unequal intervals scales provide the best test of the model of irrational, inconsistent, actors (or measures). True interval values are not in the heads (or elsewhere) of actors, and instruments to not properly reflect or capture these. Actors can at best report, and instruments can at best capture, rankings. With 12 unequal intervals, one simulates actors who report (or instruments that capture) a range of values somewhat inconsistently. Here, observed measures diverge substantially from true measures, for example, r = .71169 for NONWH. Interestingly, imperfect measurement does not invariably reduce the overall correlation coefficient; in some cases, it increases.

Multiple regression was also run to produce multiple correlation and path coefficients for 25 4-variable models specifiable for various combinations of the measurements treatments and variables. Thus dropout rate (true values), percentage nonwhite (true values and 4 rescaled value sets), and divorce rate (true values and 4 rescaled value sets) were regressed on murder rate (true values). These results are reported in Table 3.2.

As was the case with bivariate regression coefficients, some path (beta) coefficients also increased, as indicated in Table 3.2. For example, in model 5, P_{42} increases from the true value of .34991 to .63532 where only NONWH is imperfectly measured, and rise even higher (to .64950) where other variables are imperfectly measured.

TABLE 3.1

Bivariate Regression Coefficients for Perfectly and Imperfectly Measured Variables

	MURDER	DIVORCE	DROPOUT	NONWH	2 NONWH	4 NONWH	3 NONWH	5 NONWH	2 DIVORCE	3 DIVORCE	4 DIVORCE	5 DIVORCE
1 MURDER	1.00000	0.31642	0.77368	0.59078	0.51053	-0.15321	0.58226	0.80824	0.22494	0.36338	0.28118	0.34097
1 DIVORCE		1.00000	0.16605	-0.07005	-0.10591	-0.04758	-0.06338	-0.06085	0.61031	0.98296	0.55163	0.71034
1 DROPOUT			1.00000	0.44780	0.39071	-0.24551	0.44665	0.71348	0.14738	0.21799	0.21289	0.30154
1 NONWH				1.00000	0.93502	0.09888	0.99176	0.71169	-0.11412	-0.04528	-0.11749	-0.06751
2 NONWH					1.00000	0.02820	-.93415	0.69244	-0.13800	-0.08205	-0.11085	-0.11201
4 NONWH						1.00000	0.09622	-0.35450	0.01556	-0.05165	-0.10061	-0.14771
3 NONWH							1.00000	0.69806	-0.07479	-0.03942	-0.08530	-0.03490
5 NONWH								1.00000	-0.11859	-0.00846	-0.06466	-0.00943
2 DIVORCE									1.00000	0.58147	0.81343	0.86557
3 DIVORCE										1.00000	0.54031	0.69682
4 DIVORCE											1.00000	0.90088
5 DIVORCE												1.00000

TABLE 3.2
Squared Multiple Correlations and Path Coefficients

Model Number	Scaling Method DIVORCE/NONW	R² y.123	(DIVORCE) P₄₁	(NONWH) P₄₂	DROPOUT P₄₃	P₃₁	P₃₂
1	TRUE (Divorce/Nonw)	.73016	-.24524	.34991	.57627	.19839*	.46170
2	1 2	.70612	-.24512	.29516	.61754	.20978*	.41293
3	1 3	.72364	-.24096	.33709	.58311	.19514*	.45902
4	1 4	.79778	.19357	.04949*	.75148	.15472*	-.23815
5	1 5	.81972	.31044	.63532	.26885	.21024	.72627
5	2 1	.70262	.17699	.34548	.59289	.20110*	.47075
7	3 1	.73456	.25718	.35158	.56018	.23876*	.45861
8	4 1	.70993	.20212	.35941	.56970	.26922	.47943
9	5 1	.70677	.19769	.35569	.55479	.33329	.47030
10	2 2	.67684	.17038	.28508	.63718	.20520*	.41903
11	2 3	.69295	.15992	.32377	.60550	.18180*	.46025
12	2 4	.61217	.11164*	.03294*	.76531	.15124*	-.24786*
13	2 5	.79148	.25983	.64034	.27851	.23530	.74138
14	3 2	.71024	.25647	.29637	.60197	.25175*	.41137
15	4 2	.67936	.18032	.28706	.62313	.25939*	.41947
16	5 2	.68158	.19387	.29834	.59865	.34969	.42988
17	3 3	.72806	.25304	.33886	.56716	.23558*	.45591
18	3 4	.63979	.20436	.03869*	.73856	.20587*	-.23487
18	3 5	.81985	.31226	.62623	.25881	.22407	.71537
20	4 3	.70011	.18578	.33755	.58336	.25283	.46822
21	4 4	.61473	.12431*	.04548*	.75843	.19088*	-.22638*
22	4 5	.79963	.26711	.63975	.26037	.26011	.73029
23	5 3	.69709	.18075	.33397	.57011	.31752	.45733
24	5 4	.61355	.12239*	.04869*	.74873	.27119	-.20545*
25	5 5	.79504	.27889	.64950	.22618	.30838	.71638

*F is not significant at $\alpha \leqslant .05$.

With four unequal intervals, there is considerable measurement inconsistency and uncertainty. Any true underling values are greatly obscured, response options (or information) are limited, and measurement is quite imprecise. This is perhaps our best test of the model of the actor (or instrument) as essentially dumb or limited, with no inherent interval scales at hand, and with each subject potentially responding quite differently than others to a given measurement item. Here, observed statistics fluctuate greatly. Observed values have low correlations with true values, and the divergence is the greatest for any of the measurement systems. Thus the correlation of NONWH (true to observed) is only .09888. The lowest R2s occur with this measurement system, and path coefficients diverge extensively from true values. The reader may wish to inspect the tables more carefully, and may wish to undertake a similar experiment using a database of their own.

In this case, one rejects the null hypothesis that regression statistics computed on imperfectly measured variables will be equal to true values. Any "imperfect" measurement appears to induce some distortion, although the greater the imprecision, the greater the distortion. Thus, if measurement is imprecise, then the use of the parametric strategy may lead to incorrect or inaccurate results and findings. The problem, of course, is that one does not know the true values of phenomena, and hence one does not know how precise one's measures are. The measures used are typically the best there are, and if true values were knowable without measures, obviously there would be no point to engage in measurement. Thus the meaning of good results is unclear, since it is difficult to determine if one's results are accurate, or if they are merely artifacts of the measurement process and the practical decisions and knowledge of actors. Likewise, tacitly assuming the actor and/or the measure are reliable and rational may be unjustified. And if the model of the instrument as inherently imprecise, and the actor as a "dummy," is more accurate than the more rational model, then the parametric strategy and indeed the use of statistics in social science is generally problematic.

Area 3: Assessing Causal Models

Assessing causal models is a third way that second-level ethnostatistics has been put to work. The example discussed here concerns path analysis, which is a technique used to assess causal relations (paths) among variables in a theoretical model. It requires computation of all complete and partial correlations among all variables in a theoretical system. The above experiment (Gephart, 1983) provided variables and statistics appropriate to path analysis. Thus these results are used for the path analysis example presented here. The example illustrates the tacit assumptions and ad hoc decisions made in the process of constructing formal causal models. The example also shows how these decisions and assumptions, as well as assumptions and decisions made earlier in the measurement process, can effect causal models, and the theoretical and policy interpretations given these models.

The fully specified path model for the true measures of the four variables used in the experiment is given in Figure 3.1a. The lines between variables indicate the direction of causation, and the values given beside each path are the true path coefficients. Next, one must construct a parsimonious theoretical model to test with path analysis (see Figure 3.1b), since the full model is *over*specified and has zero degrees of freedom.

Constructing the parsimonious model requires certain assumptions, decisions, and ad hoc assessment criteria. For example, coefficients that are not statistically significant can be removed (Duncan, 1966). And coefficients with an absolute value of $< .05$ may be treated as not meaningful (Land, 1969), although this is an arbitrary rule and an almost superstitious use of the value ".05." Significance tests use alpha = .05 as a decision rule, but the alpha = .05 rule is merely a ritualized convention (Labovitz, 1972; Cowger, 1984).

Next, one determines whether or not the predicted correlations of the "trimmed" model "closely approximate" those of the fully specified model (Kerlinger and Pedhazur, 1973). Structural equations used to calculate predicted path coefficients, and the predicted and observed coefficients are given in Figure 3.1. The primary guideline to deletion of paths is the theory of the researcher, and the researcher must clearly employ ad hoc decision criteria to decide if the more parsimonious model is appropriate. For this illustration, the following criteria are used; for a path to be included in the model, (1) it must be statistically significant at alpha = .05, (2) it must be meaningful, that is, the coefficient must be greater than .2, and (3) the predicted correlation must not diverge more than .2 from the actual correlation (Gephart, 1983).

Path coefficients for the fully specified true model are given in row 1 of Table 3.2, and are the proper comparison for models constructed from imperfectly measured variables. Rows (models) 2 through 25

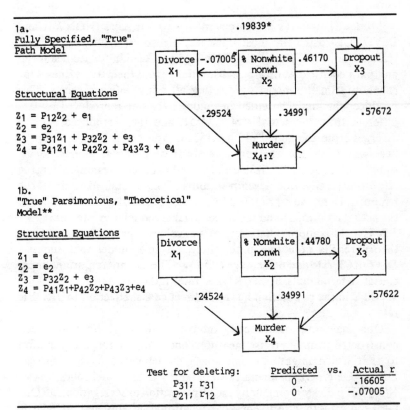

1a.
Fully Specified, "True" Path Model

Structural Equations

$$Z_1 = P_{12}Z_2 + e_1$$
$$Z_2 = e_2$$
$$Z_3 = P_{31}Z_1 + P_{32}Z_2 + e_3$$
$$Z_4 = P_{41}Z_1 + P_{42}Z_2 + P_{43}Z_3 + e_4$$

1b.
"True" Parsimonious, "Theoretical" Model**

Structural Equations

$$Z_1 = e_1$$
$$Z_2 = e_2$$
$$Z_3 = P_{32}Z_2 + e_3$$
$$Z_4 = P_{41}Z_1 + P_{42}Z_2 + P_{43}Z_3 + e_4$$

Test for deleting:	Predicted	vs.	Actual r
$P_{31}; r_{31}$	0		.16605
$P_{21}; r_{12}$	0		−.07005

Figure 3.1: Path Models for Four-Variable System.
*F is not significant at $\alpha = .05$; **Duncan's selection criteria (Duncan, 1966) are the level of meaningfulness and statistical significance of path coefficients. Hereafter, I follow him and delete all nonsignificant paths.

present the path coefficients for these imperfectly measured variables, and confirm the instability of the coefficients. For example, P41 has a true value of .24524; where it is imperfectly measured, it ranges from .31226 (model 19) to .11164 (model 12). Indeed, p32 has a true value of .46170, but becomes sizably negative in several models (4, 12, 17, 21) where the variable NONWH is measured by the least sophisticated instrument. Thus P32 goes as low as −.24786 in model 12, but also goes as high as .74138 (model 13). Clearly, construction of interval variables from ordinal data using a faulty measuring instrument leads to results that can be highly inconsistent with true values.

Model 21 involves measurement of two variables (NONWH and DIVORCE) using the most imperfect measures; 4 unequal interval scales. This model is diagrammed in Figure 3.2a in fully specified form, and path coefficients diverge substantially from their true values. One can now trim the model by deleting all nonsignificant values. This produces the model specified in Figure 3.2b. The reproduced r = 0 is different from the actual r of −.24551, and the reproduced r42 = 0 diverges from the actual r42 = −.15324. Another rule or criterion is necessary to decide whether to retain these paths; they may not be significant, but they are sizable and have theoretical meaning. Using the .2 absolute value rule developed above, P32 is retained while p42 is trimmed. Here, the reproduced (predicted) r42 = −.1899 is very close to the actual r = −.15321 and the three variable model presented in Figure 3.2c is a close approximation to actual values. The test of the original theory results in a two path, three variable model that suggests DIVORCE rate and percentage NONWHITE are not important direct causal determinants of MURDER rate, although percentage NON-WHITE in the population has an indirect causal effect on MURDER rate.

One may now theoretically interpret the model that has been constructed from imprecise measures, and compare the interpretation to that which might be made for a model based on true values. DIVORCE is perhaps an indicator of family stability and cohesiveness, NONWH indicates community racial integration or segregation, DROP-OUT indicates the effectiveness of educational systems, and MURDER represents criminality and violence in society. Social policy based on the model developed from imprecise measures might lead the social scientist to argue that a primary determinant of crime is the ineffectiveness of the educational system, which, in turn, is caused by racial strife and segregation. Racial integration does not relate directly to violent crime; only its path through the educational system effects violence in society. One might recommend, then, that (1) police budgets be increased to deal with the juvenile delinquents that the schools have turned loose (DROPOUT), (2) the educational system must be made more authoritarian to deal promptly with the matter of teaching youths to be less violent, and (3) social services spending related to the family and racial integration cannot directly effect crime or violence rates. Indeed, the 3-variable model indicates spending on social services programs is irrelevant to the crime rate.

2a. Fully Specified model

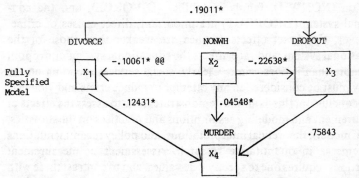

REDUCES VIA DUNCANS' STATISTICALLY SIGNIFICANT AND MEANINGFUL CRITERIA (AND MY
PRESUMPTION THAT $-.22$ is MEANINGFUL) TO

2b. Structural Equations

$$z_3 = e_4$$
$$z_4 = p_{43} z_3 + e_4$$

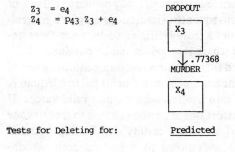

Tests for Deleting for:	Predicted	Actual
$P_{32} : r_{32}$	0	$-.24551$@@
$P_{42} : r_{42}$	0	$-.15321$@@

2c. Structural Equations

$$z_2 = e_2$$
$$z_3 = P_{32} z_z + e_3$$
$$z_4 = P_{43} z_3 + e_4$$

Tests for Deleting:	Predicted	Actual
$P_{42} : r_{42} = P_{43} P_{32}$	$-.1899$	$-.15321$

**Figure 3.2: DIVORCE and NONWH Rescaled to Four Unequal Intervals, Pure
Ordinal Scales**
***F prob. at $\alpha = .05$, path coefficient is not statistically significant;
@@From Table 3.1**

Consider again the "true" model in Figure 3.1. Here, racial segregation (NONWH), family instability (DIVORCE), and the educational system (DROPOUT) are important, direct causes of crime. However, the direct effects of race are weaker than those of the educational system, and race affects the educational system or dropout rate more than it does crime. Clearly, social services spending on the family must be considered in any attempt to reduce crime and violence.

In conclusion, this example demonstrates how to assess the effects of measurement and modeling assumptions and practices on the statistics, causal models, theoretical interpretations, and policy recommendations that emerge in quantitative research. Assessment of measurement distortions requires one to specify true values, and to contrast these with the values resulting from defective measures. This raises the issue of the generalizability of simulations of measurement imprecision effects; since there may be no true values in the supposed real world, the measured values of social science instruments may be mere artifacts of the measurement process. Consequently, simulations may lack generalizability because they construct a truly artificial world, since measurement imprecision exists only where true values can be obtained.

Yet it is commonly accepted that measurement imprecision is a fact of life in social science because measurement instruments fail to adequately convert members' meanings into precise, reliable, and valid values. If measurement is imprecise, distortions arise and can lead to incorrect or misleading interpretations of statistical results and findings. And if measurement imprecision is widespread in social research, a considerable proportion of quantitative social scientific findings may be problematic. Certain quantitative studies may have retarded rather than advanced social science knowledge, because their conclusions differ from those which would emerge from true or more accurate results. Indeed, the general use of statistics in social research is potentially problematic for these reasons. Statistics may lead the social scientist to erroneous results and conclusions, or to results for which it is difficult to establish scientific meaning. Further, even if perfect measurement could be accomplished, the researcher would necessarily be faced with interpreting and elaborating methodological rules. Thus two different researchers using the same data may produce different statistical analyses and causal models using the same statistic, because of the variability in decision practices. These problems have been suggested through the path analysis example, but they arise with any and all statistical procedures, and quantitative analyses.

The "statistics" themselves are not the problem; the issue is that statistical analyses and causal modeling cannot be undertaken independently of social constraints or practical decisions. Tacit knowledge, taken-for-granted assumptions, and ad hoc elaboration of rules always occur as qualitative features of quantitative analysis. The correspondence between events in the social world, and the theoretical concepts and measurement instruments of social science, is an ongoing problem in quantitative analysis. This correspondence is merely hidden, not addressed, by imposing interval scales and parametric statistics on social data.

4. STATISTICS AS RHETORIC

Art and Rhetoric have not been sent into perpetual exile to live outside the walls of Science and Knowledge. With or without passport, they steal back into the havens of clinical and antiseptic scholarship and operate from underground stations to lead forays into the headquarters of the enemy [Gusfield, 1981: 93].

This chapter addresses statistics as rhetoric, a third level of ethnostatistics. The concern is how to conduct research into the rhetorical or persuasive properties of statistics as literary displays locatable in scientific documents and publications.

Rhetoric is the study of all the ways of accomplishing things with language; it is the art of persuasion, or the production of an argument claiming validity for a particular audience (Gusfield, 1981; McCloskey, 1985). Rhetoric is thus a box of tools for persuaders and an antimethodology that points out what is actually done, what seems to persuade, and why. Rhetoric emphasizes that arguments do not occur in a vacuum, but are directed at specific audiences. Further, rhetoric is a rigorous endeavor involving explicitness, precision, and economy in argument. Rhetoric does not mean a "verbal shell game," as in the sense of the phrase "mere rhetoric"; all sciences are rhetorical (McCloskey, 1985).

Rhetoric provides an approach to the literary criticism of statistics, by treating statistical displays and the papers in which they are embedded as reality *sui generis*; units or objects of analysis in their own right (Gusfield, 1981: 86). Statistical displays are treated as dramatic presentations to a (public) scientific community, and their underlying frameworks analyzed. That is, scientific documents that employ statistics are conceived as "communicating devices and cultural products" (Gusfield, 1981: 84) used to persuade.

The "language of presentation" of statistical displays is a focal concern. One seeks the literary, symbolic, and linguistic techniques and methods by which the displays accomplish persuasion; the methods designed to induce belief (Gusfield, 1981: 28). This is not to assert that statistics are merely rhetoric or literature. Rather, the rhetorical perspective acknowledges that scientific documents that use statistics are major tools for reporting research. The literary style and language of the documents can be transformed into objects of study that help us understand how the construction of a factual reality rests on the proclaimed authority of statistics (Bowden, 1985).

Rhetoric leads to a concern with the textual aspects of statistics, the "productivity of language and the production of meaning" (Harari, 1979: 38). Text is a methodological field (Barthes, 1979: 74), "experienced only in an activity, a production" (p. 75). It cuts across the distinction between reading and writing (Harari, 1979: 39), and is "produced by the perpetual transformation of "another text" (p. 38). The statistic as text is transformed from a formal, complete organic whole constituted in literary appearances, into an

indefinite field in permanent metamorphosis, where language is ceaselessly at work ... a new economy in which no language is privileged over any other ... where meaning is in permanent flux and where the author is either an effect or a "guest" of the text, not its originator [Harari, 1979: 40].

The remainder of this chapter is concerned with recent rhetorical analyses of two important areas in social science: economics, and the justification of quantification. The two areas are not mutually exclusive. However, to illustrate specific topics within each of the two areas, a total of eight examples are discussed: three examples of the rhetoric of economics and five examples of the rhetoric of quantitative justification.

Area 1: The Rhetoric of Economics

McCloskey (1985) provides an extensive and sophisticated study of the rhetoric of economics; he examines a wide range of rhetorical devices used in economic literature on a variety of topics. The three brief examples here are from McCloskey; the reader may wish to consult McCloskey directly for details of these and other examples.

Example 1. McCloskey (1985: 141) initiates a study of "the rhetoric of quantification" by showing how rhetorical standards are necessary (and used implicitly) to measure the integration of markets. To assess the degree of integration of markets, one must determine "how big is big." This is the well-known problem of differentiating among the size of a numeric value, the level of statistical significance, and the theoretical meaning of the values or significant differences. The issue arises in economic arguments that measure the correlation between two parts of a market. Some economists then conclude that the market is integrated, whereas others use the same statistics to conclude it is not (McCloskey, 1985: 143). Clearly, one needs a standard to make a conclusion, and this standard is hidden for individual decision makers, who report their decisions but not the rationales. More important, any standard is embedded in a language game, and the standard lacks meaning outside the language game. McCloskey reviews the problems of developing a useful and constant standard for assessing integration, to show that it is participation in a language game, and not the value of numbers or their inherent meaning, which sets the standards and effects interpretations.

Example 2. A second example of the rhetoric of economics concerns figures of speech (*tropes*) at work in Robert Solow's classic essay on the production function $Q = A(t)f(K,L)$. The tropes include (1) metaphor, a figure of speech in that a word or phrase that literally denotes one kind of object is used in place of another to suggest a likeness or analogy (*Websters*, 1974: 722), (2) *metonymy*, letting a thing merely associated with a thing in question stand as a symbol for it (McCloskey, 1985: 84), (3) *synecdoche*, taking a part as representative of the whole (McCloskey, 1985: 84), and (4) *irony*, the use of words to express the opposite of literal meaning.

The Solow paper was analyzed by McCloskey (1985) because "the best way to show the metaphorical character of economics is to show it working in the economics apparently most far removed from literary matters" (p. 83), for example, in mathematically based papers. McCloskey justifies the significance of the selected article in terms of the quantitative nature of the topic, and the large number of citations of the paper by economists. And McCloskey himself uses synecdoche as a methodological tactic; he reprints and uses the introduction to the

Solow paper as representative of both the entire paper and econometric papers in general.

McCloskey's approach is to search the selected passage from Solow for examples of the "master tropes" or primary figures of speech displayed in the aggregate production function $Q = A(t)f(K,L)$. Metaphor is operative in the very term *aggregate production function*. The metaphor here is that the complex aspects of working life are likened to "a chalked curve on a blackboard" (McCloskey, 1985: 84). Metonymies are evident in the K and L components of the equation, where symbols associated with phenomena are left to stand for the phenomena. Thus L reduces human activity to a number of hours of work summarized by the value L (labor inputs). K "reduces the material inheritance of the workplace to a pile of shmoos" (p. 84). Synecdoche is boldly produced by Solow when he identifies A(t) with all of technical change, since a number of other things (e.g., improvements in the education of the work force) will cause the multiplier A to rise. A(t) as technical change over time is thus part of the cause of this rise, but synecdoche arises in treating it as representing the whole. Finally, Solow uses irony to persuade the reader. For example, Solow's statement: "In this day of rationally designed econometric studies and super input-output tables" (in McCloskey, 1985: 83) is ironic, in part because of the ironic use (double meaning) of the term *super* and because the audience of the paper was aware that the rationality of these studies was seriously in doubt. And in describing the paper's proposed contribution to the literature, Solow refers to "the new wrinkle I want to describe," thereby ironically understating the seriousness of his paper.

Example 3. A final example is McCloskey's (1985: 154-174) ironic deconstruction of significance tests. He notes that the lay meaning of the term *significant* leads to the universal abuse of the statistical meaning of significant results. While statistical significance is not equivalent to economic significance, McCloskey shows that numerous economists treat these as equivalent and "even the best economists, in short, overuse the statistical test of significance" (p. 172). This is established with a general analysis of 159 papers published in *American Economic Review* (see McCloskey, 1985: 169-172) and a detailed analysis of a probability sample of 10 of these papers. McCloskey also shows that most econometric texts don't mention that one cannot ascertain the validity of a hypothesis on strictly statistical grounds (p. 158). The point is not that one should abandon such tests, but that economics needs to develop standards of argument that go beyond the inconclusive ritual of hypothesize-fit-test-publish (p. 159).

In this example, McCloskey uses irony extensively, for example, by noting that while significance tests keep one from being made to look like a certain kind of fool, they don't protect against other kinds of foolishness (p. 160). And he shows that, while economists use the mathematics of sampling on a daily basis, they rarely take samples. Random sampling is necessary for the validity of inference measures. Economists typically assume, for example, that Canada's aggregate national income since 1940 is one sample of possible aggregate incomes that might have occurred. Clearly, the sample is not random and it is likely not a sample, but a population, hence the data may not meet inference assumptions. The point is that the use of tests of significance is a rhetorical accomplishment, not a technical one.

Area 2: The Rhetoric of Quantitative Justification

The constant comparative method (Glaser and Strauss, 1967; Turner, 1981) provides a strategy for the analysis of the rhetorical properties of statistics in scientific texts. The examples here are taken from Gephart (1986) and were selected because they continue and extend the earlier discussion of the parametric strategy and because they apply rhetorical analysis to methodological papers that might normally be viewed as resistant to such analyses.

The goal of the research (Gephart, 1986) was to determine how the papers used quantitative methods to produce knowledge that appeared objective, and since this objectivity is a primary defense for using quantitative methods, the task was essentially to deconstruct this objectivity. Stated differently, the goal was to discover the rhetorical practices that achieve the appearance of objectivity and hence provide the justification for quantification. (See Gephart, 1986 for further discussion of the defense for quantification implicit in parametric strategy papers.) The research thus sought to determine ways in which the "open" choices and rules of science are converted into the "closed" objectivity of publications. The investigation revealed how, despite the intent of scientific papers, the selectivity and indexicality of quantitative/statistical methods undermines the possibility that they can be truly objective.

The research involved a comparative content analysis of 16 quantitative methodological papers concerning the adequacy of the parametric strategy. The papers were selected because of their importance in the field and because, as technical or methodological papers, they are as objective and technically sophisticated as possible. In contrast to studies that simply use the parametric strategy to study social reality, the papers in this sample use technical procedures and methods to study the propriety of technical procedures themselves. And the sample was representative and meaningful, if not exhaustive, since it included research from three disciplinary domains; sociology, political science, and marketing. Further, all papers were published in internationally recognized journals, hence the literary genre was constant.

The first task was to determine a basis for comparison and analysis by using a thematic analysis similar to Garfinkel's (1967: chap. 7) analysis of methodological parameters in psychiatric patient selection studies. After carefully reading and outlining the papers, then inspecting my own summaries to discern central issues, I proposed recurrent themes common to, and constitutive of the arguments in all the papers. The important themes or parameters they seemed to have in common were as follows: (1) an author or authors, (2) a location (journal in which they were published), (3) reasons for using the parametric strategy, (4) rationale for the study, (5) study objectives, (6) comments on measurement, (7) data, (8) true levels of measurement for independent and dependent variables, (9) measures of distortion, (10) scoring systems or methods of transforming values, (11) results, and (12) conclusions.

Using several very large sheets of paper, I created a comparative table where each parameter was a column, and each study a different row. Studies were sequentially ordered in terms of publication date, from the earliest study to the latest. The next step was to exhaustively search all the articles to find all examples of each of the parameters or themes. Essentially, direct quotations from each study concerning each parameter were copied into the table, and the page number noted. Where quotes were too lengthy, or discussion too segmented to reproduce as a quotation, brief summaries were used. However, the use of quotes was generally possible; over 95% of the cells in this table contain only direct quotes. And where the same points were made multiple times in a given article, redundant statements were noted by page number, but not completely recorded. This procedure provided the content for comparative analysis. Deconstructing the papers in this manner re-contextualized their content as "standard" themes, which were now placed adjacent to one another on the same sheet(s) of paper.

The next task was to inspect similarities and differences among studies, to surface insights into literary practices that produced each paper's sense of objectivity. Comparing down rows of the table within a given column shows the historical evolution of that theme across papers, since the studies were ordered temporally. Comparison across columns within a row shows the contrasts across themes for a given study. And comparing different rows for all or some subset of columns provides a way of assessing similarities and differences between particular studies. I wanted to see how studies did similar things differently, for example, used dissimilar scoring systems to produce an assessment of the same statistic. The comparative cells thus made explicit and visible the selectivity of each study, since the other studies evidenced alternatives that are available. And I also wanted to see how different studies did different things similarly, that is, to find examples of dissimilar practices or procedures that were treated as similar.

The research was concept and theory driven, and theory constructive (Glaser and Strauss, 1967). Armed with an outline of concepts and findings from social studies of science, I searched both the thematic comparison table and the papers themselves to find examples of concepts and ideas, such as selectivity, indexicality, taken-for-granted assumptions, and the irreplicability of methods. As examples were located, they were used to elaborate and extend the meaning of concepts and thereby show how they fit the issues of measurement and statistics. This was an iterative process: I tried to propose themes or hypotheses of increasing generality, and then reinspect data to ensure that multiple examples of each concept were available, and that each emergent theme reflected the scope and range of the examples subsumed by the theme.

As themes and examples began to accumulate, a first draft of an analysis of the papers was written. The organizing themes or headings in this draft were very close to the conventional organizational themes of the papers themselves: rationale and objectives, measurement theory, methods, results, and conclusions. Within each theme, I traced the evolution of concerns across the history of the area, that is, across the rows of the comparative table. The draft presents numerous specific examples of key concepts, such as practical reasoning, and the constructed nature of statistics, and the draft discusses substantive issues that emerged.

The themes were continuously revised across later drafts of the manuscript. The tactic of listing all good examples of a theme was replaced with the strategy of selecting representative examples. As this occurred, the implications of the examples—originally discussed at the end of each section—became the initial assertions of the section. Essentially, the text moved from a pattern of "here are the examples, then here is the conclusion" to one of "here is the conclusion, and these are key illustrative examples." This cycling back of conclusions to premises is an integral part of grounded theory construction (Glaser and Strauss, 1967) and it crystallized the themes ultimately used as organizational headings for the final (published) draft of the manuscript. Below, I discuss five examples of how the rhetorical analysis was undertaken, and the conclusions that emerged.

Example 1: Surfacing the practice of next-stepping. Comparative table columns concerned with rationales and objectives provided evidence that the rationale for each paper was previous research in the area. Each paper referenced past papers and located itself as a product flowing from the implicit needs and explicit concerns of past studies—a scientific community. For example, Labovitz (1967) warranted his seminal paper in terms of general practices. Labovitz (1970) located itself as a next step after Labovitz (1967), and, by 1973, Martin (1973) referenced 6 studies as a context for warranting present research. The meaning of past research was not stable or self-evident but was given specific or unique meaning in each subsequent publication. For example, Labovitz (1970) suggested that Labovitz (1967) demonstrated the parametric strategy was appropriate, whereas Henkel (1970) argued that Labovitz (1967) demonstrated the strategy was deficient.

This suggested how each paper used past literature to create its own reasons for existence. I gave this practice a general label, "next stepping," that is, transforming past papers into resources or reasons for undertaking this "next" paper. The practice of "next stepping" disguises the fact that the parametric strategy is used for the simple practical reason that social science has data that require transformation if arbitrarily preferred statistics are to be used. Next-stepping disguised this practicality because each paper referenced the interests of previous papers and thus created a tradition external to itself by finding next steps, indicated by others, that could be undertaken. These next steps emerged from the tension each paper established in stating its rationale in its initial pages. Authors constructed a history of emerging scientific literature where certain *lacunae* (holes) exist, waiting to be filled. These holes, or literary lacunae, are those features that "have not been investigated" (Martin, 1978: 304) in previous papers. For example, O'Brien (1982: 145) stated, "Our results fill in several gaps and extend these earlier studies." Thus through construction of "obvious omissions" in the field that any sensible researcher can see, the omissions were given an objective character. By filling a generally evident hole in the literature, the papers avoided having a focus that appeared arbitrary or idiosyncratic; the papers thus came to address shared, external and obvious—that is, objective—concerns.

The data in the table also revealed how authors used next stepping practices by interpreting the choices, techniques, and findings of previous research in terms of the interests of their current paper. Authors recontextualized and reinterpreted selections of previous research and thereby questioned the adequacy of previous papers. Such attacks were generally subtle—what Knorr-Cetina (1981) terms "dis-simulative textual practices." For example, following Gusfield (1981) and Knorr-Cetina (1981), I examined the "voice" of the authors, and noted that they depersonalized their attacks by the tactic of writing in an impersonal style and tone; for example, "one side argues . . . " (Bollen and Barb, 1981). These phrases sound neutral and dispassionate, and the author seems disembodied or removed from the issues. Authors also referred to general contexts, common knowledge, and externally available criteria for assessing adequacy. This infers an objective character to the criticisms and themes of their papers. Typically, authors did not assault or insult one another explicitly. Rather, research papers created their contribution by defeating others in an implicit guerrilla campaign of insinuation and innuendo (Knorr-Cetina, 1981) about the competence of others to produce objective knowledge in a scientifically warranted manner.

Example 2: Finding ad hoc features of measurement theory. The term *measurement* is widely used as a technical warrant for quantitative research. Initially, I expected PS papers, as methodological contributions, would employ sophisticated models of measurement and would use or reference some general scientific theory of measurement. Instead, the statements made concerning measurement reflected authors' taken-for-granted understandings, beliefs, and knowledge. These seemed at best to be implicit, elusive theories of measurement, revealed in piecemeal assertions fashioned to serve the particular literary concerns of each paper. Indeed, the comparative table showed that different measurement models were constructed in each different paper, and that authors' reasons for using the models were stated in terms of practical interests and beliefs.

For example, Labovitz (1967) states that the parametric strategy is appropriate where measurement is not well developed. This is a statement of beliefs that assumes an implicit theory of measurement: Strict adherence to "level of measurement" requirements is impractical because different scales of measurement are difficult to distinguish. Other examples of tacit, practical theories of measurement are provided by Boyle (1970) and Kim (1975), who believed that the use of poor measures will somehow improve measurement. Thus the comparative analysis indicated that the strategy's utility was preserved in these papers through ad hoc use of implicit theories of measurement, and through selectively employing and interpreting measurement concepts in ways that justified or supported the authors' beliefs.

Use of persuasive rhetoric and implicit theories of the meaning of measures were also important textual practices evident in PS papers. Measurement models were used as implicit resources to warrant authors' beliefs, and to criticize the beliefs and tactics of others. For example, Henkel (1975: 11) "defeated" Labovitz's claims with ad hoc arguments such as, "It is not clear in what sense even univariate statistics assuming an interval level of measurement are interpretable when applied to data scaled at less than an interval level." This is a provocative statement, but it fails to provide or suggest a theory of how to interpret statistics, that is, a theory of the meaning of measures. Similarly, quoting Hays (1963: 71-72), Henkel argued, "If nonsense is put into the mathematical system, nonsense is sure to come out" (p. 9). This is again a rhetorically provocative assertion that avoids mention of an explicit model or theory of measurement.

The comparative table also showed how measurement models evolved into increasingly elaborate technical resources over the history of the PS papers, as new technical distinctions were introduced to justify each succeeding paper. For example, Labovitz's (1967) discussion of measurement treated measurement theory as a rudimentary technical resource, primarily level of measurement assumptions and error involving differences between true and observed scores. Kim (1975) developed a diagrammatic model of measurement and introduced the concept of ordered polytomies (tied ranks) to undermine the conclusions of previous studies.

A particularly revealing example of the technical evolution of measurement concepts is provided by O'Brien's insightful research on measurement error. "Grouping errors" (O'Brien, 1981a) emerged as a key measurement concept, but a *general theory of measurement* was elusive. The term was first used in O'Brien (1981a), but was not linked to any general measurement theory or to other literature since O'Brien did not reference any previous discussions or uses of the term. Later, O'Brien (1981b: 606-607) defined two types of errors: *transformation errors* and *categorization errors*. These terms originated in personal communications between O'Brien and Hensler and Stipak, and this source was indicated in a footnote (1981b: 606, n. 4), not in a general or explicit theory. By 1981, *grouping error* had become a general term subsuming transformation and categorization error. Later papers by other authors devised their own meanings for measurement terms. Thus the comparative table helped me to ascertain that technical measurement terms such as *categorization error* and *grouping error* acquired textually unique—that is, indexical—meanings. Between papers, the terms were not interchangeable, and their meaning in individual papers was tailored to preserve the coherence of each paper. Measurement models evidenced ad hoc characteristics, were constructed uniquely in different studies, and were injected into research at those points in the text when it was necessary to provide a technical rationale for the manipulations of the researcher.

More importantly, the comparative table showed that measurement theories and concepts did not refer to measurement activities, what people do when doing measurement. Measurement discussions did not discuss or justify, for example, the fact one can set category values either before or after handing out a questionnaire. And the discussions did not explain or address how subjects interpret items. Rather, the measurement theory that emerged seemed to be a curious blend of belief, practical reasoning, and mathematical descriptions. Following Cicourel (1964), this was considered measurement theory by fiat, that is, measurement theory in these papers was an ad hoc resource that failed to describe social and interpretative aspects inherent in measurement activities and practices.

Example 3: Substantiating the inherent nonreplicability of methods. Replicability of methods refers to the extent that abstract methodological procedures can be used by a knowledgeable researcher to do the same study or analysis again in exactly the same way. If methodological rules and statistical procedures are indexical, quantitative methods and results would be expected to be inherently nonreplicable; each context is unique and requires unique translations of the general procedures. To establish evidence related to this theme, I again searched the data for evidence that papers did not attempt, or were unable, to replicate previous studies and methods. Further, I reread methodological passages, and sought to make explicit all the steps and activities I would have to undertake to replicate the studies. Then I again examined the comparative table and the original studies to determine any information that I needed for these replications, but that was not given in the studies.

For example, procedures used in PS papers to create data, scoring systems, and measures of distortion were "described" by references to general methodological rules and formulae. PS papers assumed the reader could undertake these standard and general methodological practices. Thus Martin (1975) described the generation of his data by simply referencing a statistics text where the formula for the bivariate normal distribution appears. This assumes the reader is familiar with integral calculus, probability density functions, and use of computers to generate the 1,000 values that were somehow generated from this formula. The reader is not given enough information to replicate this procedure; for example, the method or formula(e) for calculating these values is unmentioned. And the comparative table also revealed that Martin's (1975) rather long (three paragraph) statement on the details of the distribution was reduced in Martin (1978) to three paragraphs and a reference to Martin (1975) as the source of the procedure, thereby further glossing and objectifying the method. These practices thus concealed the inherent choices made in using the procedure.

Stating procedures in a quasi-passive voice and linking them to shared knowledge was another practice the studies used to disguise procedural choices. For example, O'Brien (1979: 853) stated, "This simulation follows the rules outlined by Labovitz (1970: 517)," and noted a version of fortran was used to generate the assigned scores, "These values were then correlated" (p. 853). This type of language standardizes and externalizes procedures as part of common scientific knowledge. And it removes the author's personal involvement in the creation of study specific methods.

Nonthematization of the indexical aspects of procedures was an important practice for disguising nonreplicable aspects of methods. This nonthematization further limited the replicability of the papers. For example, given O'Brien's (1979, 1981a, 1982) procedures, one is unable to reproduce the actual values used, since these were randomly generated and were not given in the study. Another random sample would produce different values; the same rules could thus generate different data sets and possibly different results. And one would not know the hidden selections, unmentioned in the procedure, which were made by the researcher. Thus, to replicate these quantitative methods, one must presume—often with little reason—that the procedures used were of some particular "standard" form.

General procedures were clearly indexical—they had to be transformed into study-specific practices within each research venture. Yet description of specific activities was not undertaken in PS papers, and no mention was made of idiosyncratic or situation-specific troubles each researcher faced in using general procedures. I therefore concluded that while the papers reported quantitative data as objective, replicable evidence to support their conclusions, the procedures used were inherently nonreplicable because the papers glossed and disguised the inherent indexicality of general methodological rules and practices. The papers idealized research and did not provide adequate information on the practical activities that produced the quantitative results and conclusions.

Example 4: Uncovering indexicality in the meaning of numbers. PS papers, like other quantitative research, report results in tables of numbers that contain or summarize observed values for the variables measured in the research. Adjacent to these tables of numbers one finds verbal, nonquantitative remarks that refer to the tables to highlight and interpret the numbers. Results also appear as an object of discussion in the final section of the papers, generally entitled "conclusions."

I was concerned with understanding how numbers are given meaning, when they are transformed from results into findings. I expected significance tests to be resources for constructing meaning but found they played only a minor role in interpreting numbers. Next, I attempted to compare (both within and between papers) the quantitative (numeric) values constituting results with the qualitative (verbal) interpretation given to these as "findings." Thus, again using the comparative table as well as the original studies, I searched for particular values (e.g., r values, such as .9) and the corresponding verbal interpretations (e.g., "high" correlation). I tried to keep values constant and compare different words used, or to keep words constant and compare different values used, for example, all words used to describe correlations of .9 or higher. This was generally successful, but there were also some problems in comparing the interpretations given in specific studies, since each paper uses not only different words and values, but also somewhat different statistical procedures. Some papers use single r's, others used average r's or differences, and so on.

This suggested that the use of different statistics by each study was a practice that ensured that the studies were in certain ways inherently incomparable; there were a number of meanings for the meaning of a number. Also, given the number of numbers reported in a given study for which meanings might be provided, not all values or results were explicitly explained or interpreted in the scientific paper. Much vagueness or indexicality remained, since a number of meanings were unspecified for a number of numbers.

Reflecting on the words used to describe values, it became clear that the general practice for interpreting quantitative results is to link adjectives and adverbs to numbers to thereby transform the numbers into meaningful results. For example, PS papers used adjectives such as small, slight, substantial, high, and/or stable to describe values. These adjectives were often coupled to adverbs, for greater precision, for example, "usually or highly stable." Relations between values were described in terms of fairly good agreement, essentially no difference, and differences that are small. Different values were termed unequal, very unequal, almost equal, close, and a substantial drop. Errors are small, slight, and minor; and "substantial" or "a great deal of distortion" is found.

Terms that are similar were observed to be applied to different numeric values and similar values were linked to different descriptive terms. Indeed, the value one author considered "substantial" was often the same or less than .1 discrepant from what another author labeled "relatively small." For example, in one PS paper, correlations between true and measured values that diverge .10 or less from one another are labeled "exceedingly high" (Labovitz, 1970: 520). A later paper that contests these results interprets correlations that diverge .034 to .083 from one another as showing great risk of error (Henry, 1982), that is, the correlations are low. Similarly, I claimed that path coefficients that diverge $< .01$ from true values cause "substantial distortion" (Gephart, 1983), whereas Johnson and Creech (1983: 403-405) claim path coefficients that diverge up to .038 are "quite close. . . . the differences are not of sufficient magnitude to lead to markedly different substantive interpretations." Meaning was not inherent in numbers, but was indexical; meaning was accomplished by terms used to describe and interpret numbers, and by the contexts in which these descriptions were embedded.

Example 5: Tracking the indexicality of numbers in conclusions. The final issue I addressed was the way results were used to produce conclusions. The data in the comparative table clearly showed that in the conclusions (final) sections, the terms *results* and *findings* were used frequently and repeatedly, but specific values were seldom given. The terms thus became a gloss that reified the meaning of numbers. For example, "the results presented above should be quite sobering" (O'Brien, 1981a: 1156). Further, I was able to find many specific inconsistencies in the data or statistics that might weaken the arguments, such as some low correlations in a set of correlations that were generally termed high. This gloss of results and findings was used when authors discussed general trends; it allowed them to ignore specific inconsistencies in the data or statistics that might weaken their argument. Thus differences in conclusions of the studies appeared to be due to interpretations constructed for the numbers, and did not derive from the absolute values themselves. This gloss of results was thus an important interpretive practice used to fulfill the rationale for a given paper. Glossing results ignored or hid any equivocal or inconsistent numbers that might contradict or confuse the contribution.

The results and conclusions were not products of the inherent properties of numbers nor of the rule bound translation of numeric values into verbal interpretations. There were a range of terms available for describing and interpreting quantitative results. And there were no explicit scientific rules for applying these terms. Researchers used terms in a sensible manner that depended on the context of use, and on both commonsense and technical criteria. Thus glossing practices converted results into conclusions and resolved the problem of the open meaning of the values of variables. Numbers were selectively given a verbal meaning consistent with authors' stated purposes for undertaking a paper, and with other aspects of the text in which results and conclusions were embedded.

5. SUMMARY AND CONCLUSIONS

Literature as well as criticism—the difference between them being delusive—is condemned (or privileged) to be forever the most rigorous and, consequently, the most unreliable language in terms of which man names and modifies himself [de Man, 1979: 140].

This final chapter summarizes the implications of the three levels of ethnostatistics described in the volume. Next, the general implications and future uses of ethnostatistics are discussed. The chapter concludes by indicating how ethnostatistics provides integrative methods for science.

First-level ethnostatistics is the scientific observation of the cultures of quantitative social science. Ethnographic methods provide thick descriptions of the interesting work lives of quantitative professionals. The methods are used to track and view more clearly the complex and elegant knowledge construction activities involved in quantification and they thus make visible the social processes involved in producing a statistic. The ethnographic data that emerge support the development of a truly social theory of social measurement (Cicourel, 1964) grounded in the actual activities and meanings of the natives who do measurement, and not simply in a priori techniques, prescriptions, or official methodological goals. A social theory of measurement can provide the basis for more adequately understanding, legitimating, demystifying, and using quantitative measures. Indeed, the point is not to force abandonment of measurement (Cicourel, 1964), but to improve measurement by investigating the actual behaviors that make up measurement.

Second-level ethnostatistics puts statistics to work testing and assessing the assumptions, social aspects, and limits of statistics. This embeds the problem of technical accomplishment in the broader sphere of social life. By offering a critical view of statistics, the situational effectiveness and adequacy of statistics are more clearly discerned. Indeed, an important use of second-level ethnostatistics is simulating the implications of taken-for-granted assumptions and ritualistic practices that have been preserved because one cannot test their utility using real data in the real world; such practices have been impervious to empirical attack. Simulations thus provide insights and quantitative data concerning the tacit assumptions and ad hoc methodological practices that emerge when statistics are put to work. By showing where statistics are appropriate or inappropriate, problems that are resolvable can be addressed, and uses that entail unsolvable problems can be abandoned. Second-level ethnostatistics thus provides for the rhetorical use of statistics in reasoned attacks on empty methodological rituals (Labovitz, 1972; Cowger, 1984).

Third-level ethnostatistics puts rhetorical methods to work deconstructing statistical presentations in scientific texts. This provides critiques of statistical research and reveals how statistics are constructed in artful literary displays used to persuade others about the truth, objectivity, and legitimacy of scientific knowledge. Understanding the rhetoric of statistics can lead to improved clarity and quality in scientific reports by suggesting literary techniques to improve the rhetoric. Further, statistics may advance knowledge more by providing metaphors for structuring and organizing data (information) than by providing ways for deciding among facts. Conceiving of statistics as metaphors encourages the search for statistical procedures that provide for more interesting and insightful metaphors. This provides an alternative to the conventional practice of selecting techniques that lead to more interpretable results or that require higher levels of measurement. The point is that it is important to understand the metaphorical character and uses of statistics, but to avoid reifying the statistics. An insightful metaphor with limits that are well appreciated is more useful in advancing science than is the hidden reification of implicit metaphors and their transformation into tautological theory.

Future Recommendations

Several recommendations for future methodological practices and opportunities emerge from ethnostatistics. First, there is an opportunity to more adequately preserve actors' meanings by developing alternative and broader forms of variables. Strictly speaking, a variable is something that varies. Consider words and talk as potential variables. The substance of what is said or written is subject to vary across different speakers, settings, and occasions. The substantive details of naturally occurring activities can be preserved in transcripts and written descriptions of action. These descriptions, and indeed any texts, documents or character strings (e.g., from documents, transcripts, or field notes) can be transformed into text variables by chunking or segmenting the text into strips (Agar, 1986). Database managers (relational database software) allow complex relational operations to be performed on text variables, permit rapid searches and manipulations of the information, and thus offer new possibilities for potentially powerful and exhaustive comparisons of text data. For example, in a relational database, each strip (e.g., one paragraph) can be treated as one column of one row of a database table, that is, as a variable since the content of each chunk varies. Thus the comparative tables used in deconstruction of the parametric strategy (chap. 4; Gephart, 1986) could be set up as database tables. Text content or strip variables preserve verbal meanings and also encourage production of other variables, some of which are naturally and inherently quantifiable. For example, in documentary analysis, one finds page and line numbers, dates, and times. These are inherently interval variables that occur naturally in recognizable commonsense forms. Another possibility is to integrate statistical data with other forms of variables in broader database designs.

Second, the conduct of quantitative social research can be improved if researchers accept that transforming the level of measurement of variables is risky. If possible, transformations should be avoided and, in all cases, the researcher should critically question the implications of the transformations. Where possible and relevant, the transformations should be explicitly reported, and the reasons and rationales discussed. And where transformations occur, the researcher should compare results of the transformed variables to results of analyses of the variables measured at their minimum level. If the results for transformed variables are substantially different than results from the initial measures, the transformations should be considered problematic. One might then wish to analyze variables that have not been transformed, and to use alternative statistics, such as nonparametrics, consistent with the level of measurement achieved prior to transformations. Indeed, while nonparametric statistics are widely taught, they are seldom used and one implication of this volume is that nonparametrics be given a larger role in future quantitative research.

Third, research should be theory or concept driven, and not driven by arbitrary or conventional rules of significance, or meaning. The general direction of trends in data and the overall pattern of results are more important than levels of significance, or specific coefficients. Thus the theoretical relevance of the data, and not the statistical significance or size of coefficients should be emphasized in research reports.

Fourth, the researcher should not expect or pretend that statistical rules are explicit and complete guides to the methodological process. The researcher should expect to undertake ad hoc and post hoc interpretations and elaborations of rules. Where these are interesting or have proved useful, they could be reported in research publications, or in separate methodological papers, thereby becoming public contributions to the improvement of research, rather than private skeletons in quantitative closets. Important contributions arise from extending methodologies beyond current limits, as well as by simply using methods within their limits.

Fifth, keeping a record of key decisions made in the research process will help in identifying important assumptions. Whenever possible, the tacit assumptions that are made in the research process should be empirically investigated and tested. These tests will help substantiate research methods. This, of course, is a primary task for ethnostatistics, and one might expect reports on these activities to be separate from reports on the original quantitative research in which they were identified. Finally, the assumptions to be investigated and tested must include not only technical/statistical assumptions such as level of measurement, but also the social features that are implied or assumed in the process of doing statistics.

Integrative Methods

The issues raised here, and the opportunities they provide, cut across disciplines. Addressing the opportunities may lead to an integrative, transdisciplinary perspective on research methods and knowledge. Rather than closing the dialogue among the sciences (social, natural, and administrative), this volume provides common ethnostatistical issues as a basis for expanding transdisciplinary dialogue. Further, the methods discussed in the volume provide rationales and means for qualitative social scientists to study quantitative methods, and for quantitative scientists to study qualitative methods. The methods discussed are not a panacea for the ills of social science, but they do provide some proven alternatives to common practices and issues. And they provide another way of exploring the implications of the dissolution of the distinction between the two sciences, social and natural (Knorr-Cetina, 1983).

The methods have led us full circle. In observing scientific activities directly (first-level ethnostatistics), one is exposed to the savage meaning of methods and the tacit assumptions that underlay them. This can provide a basis for testing the assumptions and features in second-level ethnostatistical research. The ability to actually test these assumptions introduces a level of reflexivity not available in social studies of natural science that take for granted that issues of technical or methodological adequacy are decidable only by the native scientists who are somehow distinct from the observers. And third-order studies provide a way of investigating the products and processes of all types of research, including third-level studies themselves. Rhetorical analyses of statistics and science thus introduce another meaningful form of reflexive inquiry.

In general, ethnostatistical methods allow one to track statistical, scientific knowledge across contexts and situations, and to explore science at three levels that are mutually relevant but analytically separable. Integrative research that employs all three levels of ethno-statistics simultaneously or in sequence will thus provide a multifaceted approach to the study of statistics and will complement the common view of statistics as self-contained technical tools. Further, these research methods can be used to track the micro production of macro phenomena, as well as to reveal the simultaneity of micro and macro concerns in everyday micro settings (Cicourel, 1981).

Finally, the literary concept of textuality is an important tool for integration of different methods and disciplines. Literature must come to balance mathematics as a fundamental disciplinary basis for science. The reason is that a basic aspect of scientific methods is the production of a textual description of the world (Sacks, 1963). That is, all methods transform observations and experiences into textual descriptions. For example, recording a conversation and then producing a transcript converts the conversation into a textual description. Similarly, in converting events into tables of numbers, the events are reconstituted as textual productions. Scientific analysis proceeds from and returns to the textual descriptions of events, and not the events themselves, since the events per se vanish with the perishing occasions in which they are measured. Thus one can turn to the textuality of science as an integrative method and topic; it is common to all forms of science, because science cannot proceed without it.

REFERENCES

ACOCK, A. and J. D. MARTIN (1974) "The undermeasurement controversy: should ordinal data be treated as interval?" Sociology and Social Research 58: 427-433.

AGAR, M. (1986) Speaking of Ethnography. Newbury Park, CA: Sage.

BARTHES, R. (1979) "From work to text," pp. 73-81 in J. V. Harari (ed.) Textual Strategies: Perspectives in Post-Structuralist Criticism. Ithaca, NY: Cornell University Press.

BECKER, H. S. (1963) Outsiders: Studies in the Sociology of Deviance. New York: Free Press.

BIJKER, W. E., T. P. HUGHES, and T. PINCH (1987) The Social Construction of Technological Systems. Cambridge: MIT Press.

BITTNER, E. (1973) "Objectivity and realism in sociology," pp. 109-125 in G. Psathas (ed.) Phenomenological Sociology. New York: John Wiley.

BLALOCK, H. (1961) "Correlation and causality: the multivariate case." Social Forces 39: 246-251.

BLALOCK, H. (1972) Social Statistics. New York: McGraw-Hill.

BOGDAN, R. and M. KSANDER (1980) "Policy data as a social process: a qualitative approach to quantitative data." Human Organization 39: 302-309.

BOLLEN, K. and K. BARB (1981) "Pearson's r and coarsely categorized measures." American Sociological Review 46: 232-239.

BOWDEN, G. (1985) "The social construction of validity in estimates of US crude oil reserves." Social Studies of Science 15: 207-240.

BOYLE, R. P. (1970) "Path analysis and ordinal data." American Journal of Sociology 75: 461-480.

CAVAN, S. (1966) Liquor License: An Ethnography of Bar Behavior. Chicago: Aldine.

CHURCHILL, L. (1971) "Ethnomethodology and measurement." Social Forces 50: 182-191.

CICOUREL, A. V. (1964) Method and Measurement in Sociology. New York: Free Press.

CICOUREL, A. V. (1974) Theory and Method in a Study of Argentine Fertility. New York: John Wiley.

CICOUREL, A. V. (1974) "Introduction," pp. 1-16 in Cicourel et. al., Language Use and School Performance.

CICOUREL, A. V. (1980) "Three models of discourse analysis: the role of social structure." Discourse Processes 3: 101-132.

CICOUREL, A. V. (1981) "Notes on the integration of micro- and macro-levels of analysis," pp. 51-80 in K. Knorr-Cetina and A. V. Cicourel (eds.) Advances in Social Theory and Methodology. London: Routledge & Kegan Paul.

CICOUREL, A. V., K. H. JENNINGS, S.H.M. JENNINGS, K.C.W. LEITER, R. MacKAY, H. MEHAN, and D. R. ROTH (1973) Language Use and School Performance. New York: Academic Press.

68

CICOUREL, A. V. and J. KITSUSE (1963) The Educational Decision Makers. Indianapolis: Bobbs-Merrill.

COWGER, C. D. (1984) "Statistical significance tests: scientific ritualism or scientific method?" pp. 358-372 in Social Service Review. Chicago: University of Chicago Press.

CULLER, J. (1982) On Deconstruction: Theory and Criticism after Structuralism. Ithaca, NY: Cornell University Press.

de MAN, P. (1979) "Semiology and rhetoric," pp. 121-140 in J. Harari (ed.) Textual Strategies: Perspectives in Post-Structuralist Criticism. Ithaca, NY: Cornell University Press.

DUNCAN, O. D. (1966) "Path analysis: sociological examples." American Journal of Sociology. 72: 1-16.

DURKHEIM, E. (1967) Suicide. New York: Free Press.

ELLIOT, H. C. (1974) "Similarities and differences between science and common sense," pp. 21-26 in R. Turner (ed.) Ethnomethodology. Markham, Ontario: Penguin.

EMERSON, R. M. (1969) Judging Delinquents: Context and Process in Juvenile Court. Chicago: Aldine.

EMERSON, R. M. (1981) "On last resorts." American Journal of Sociology 87: 1-22.

EMERSON, R. M. (1983) Contemporary Field Research. Boston: Little, Brown.

FEYERABEND, P. (1975) Against Method. London: Verso.

GARFINKEL, H. (1967) Studies in Ethnomethodology. Englewood Cliffs, NJ: Prentice-Hall.

GARFINKEL, H., M. LYNCH, and E. LIVINGSTONE (1981) "The work of a discovering science construed with materials from the optically discovered pulsar." Philosophy of Social Science 11: 131-158.

GEERTZ, C. (1973) The Interpretation of Cultures. New York: Basic Books.

GEPHART, R. P. (1978) "Status degradation and organizational succession: an ethnomethodological analysis." Administrative Science Quarterly 28.

GEPHART, R. P. (1979) Making Sense of Succession. Ph.D. Dissertation, University of British Columbia.

GEPHART, R. P. (1983) "Multiple R, 'The Parametric Strategy' and measurement imprecision." Sociological Perspectives 26: 473-500.

GEPHART, R. P. (1986) "Deconstructing the defense for quantification in social science: a content analysis of journal articles on the parametric strategy." Qualitative Sociology 9: 126-144.

GILBERT, N. and M. MULKAY (1980) "Contexts of scientific discourse: social accounting in experimental papers," pp. 269-294 in K. Knorr-Cetina et al. (eds.) The Social Process of Scientific Investigation: Sociology of Sciences Yearbook. Dordrecht: D. Reidel.

GLASER, B. G. and A. STRAUSS (1967) The Discovery of Grounded Theory. Chicago: Aldine.

GOFFMAN, E. (1959) The Presentation of Self in Everyday Life. New York: Doubleday.

GOFFMAN, E. (1961) Asylums. Garden City, NY: Doubleday.

GOFFMAN, E. (1963) Stigma. Englewood Cliffs, NJ: Prentice-Hall.

GOULD, S. J. (1981) The Mismeasure of Man. New York: W. W. Norton.

GUBRIUM, J. F. and D. R. BUCKHOLDT (1979) "Production of hard data in human service institutions." Pacific Sociological Review 22: 115-136.

GUSFIELD, J. (1976) "The literary rhetoric of science: comedy and pathos in drinking driver research." American Sociological Review 1: 16-34.

GUSFIELD, J. (1981) The Culture of Public Problems: Drinking-Driving and the Symbolic Order. Chicago: University of Chicago Press.

GUTTMAN, L. (1977) "What is not what in statistics." Statistician 26: 81-107.

GUTTMAN, L. (1982) "What is not what in theory construction," pp. 331-348 in Social Structure and Behavior: Essays in Honor of William Hamilton Sewell. New York: Academic Press.

HAMMERSLEY, M. and P. ATKINSON (1983) Ethnography: Principles in Practice. London: Tavistock.

HARARI, J. V. (1979) Textual Strategies: Perspectives in Post-Structuralist Criticism. Ithaca, NY: Cornell University Press.

HENKEL, R. E. (1975) "Part-whole correlations and the treatment of ordinal and quasi-interval data as interval data." Pacific Sociological Review 18: 3-26.

HENRY, F. (1982) "Multivariate analysis and ordinal data." American Sociological Review 47: 299-307.

HENSLER, C. and B. STIPAK (1979) "Estimating interval scale values for survey item response categories." American Journal of Political Science 18: 3-26.

JACOBS, J. (1979) "Burp-seltzer? I never use it: an in-depth look at market research," pp. in H. S. Schwartz and J. L. Jacobs, Qualitative Sociology: a Method to the Madness. New York: Free Press.

JOHNSON, D. and J. CREECH (1983) "Ordinal measures in multiple indicator models: a simulation study of categorization error." American Sociological Review 48: 398-407.

KERLINGER, F. N. and E. J. PEDHAZUR (1973) Multiple Regression in Behavioral Research. New York: Holt, Rinehart, & Winston.

KIM, J. (1975) "Multivariate analysis of ordinal variables." American Journal of Sociology 81: 261-298.

KITSUSE, J. V. and A. CICOUREL (1963) "A note on the uses of official statistics." Social Problems 11: 131-139.

KNORR-CETINA, K. D. (1981) The Manufacture of Knowledge: An Essay on the Constructivist and Contextual Nature of Science. Oxford: Pergamon.

KNORR-CETINA, K. D. (1983) "New developments in science studies: the ethnographic challenge." Canadian Journal of Sociology: 153-177.

KUHN, T. S. (1962) The Structure of Scientific Revolutions. Chicago: University Press.

KUNDA, G. (1986) Engineering Culture: Culture and Control in a High-Tech Organization. Ph.D. dissertation, Massachusetts Institute of Technology.

LABOVITZ, S. (1967) "Some observations on measurement and statistics." Social Forces 46: 151-160.

LABOVITZ, S. (1970) "The assignment of numbers to rank order categories." American Sociological Review 35: 515-524.

LABOVITZ, S. (1972) "Statistical usage in sociology: sacred cows and ritual." Sociological Methods and Research 1: 13-37.

LABOVITZ, S. and R. HAGEDORN (1971) Introduction to Social Research. New York: McGraw-Hill.

LAND, K. C. (1969) "Principles of path analysis," pp. 3-37 in E. F. Borgatta (ed.) Sociological Methodology, 1969. San Francisco: Jossey-Bass.

LATOUR, B. (1987) Science in Action. Cambridge, MA: Harvard University Press.

LATOUR, B. and S. WOOLGAR (1979) Laboratory Life: The Social Construction of Scientific Facts. Newbury Park, CA: Sage.

LATOUR, B. and S. WOOLGAR (1986) Laboratory Life: The Construction of Scientific Facts. Princeton, NJ: Princeton University Press.

70

LEITER, K. (1980) A Primer in Ethnomethodology. New York: Oxford.
LIEBERSON, S. M. (1985) Making it Count. Berkeley: University of California Press.
LYNCH, M. E. (1982) "Technical work and critical inquiry: investigations in a scientific laboratory." Social Studies of Science 12: 499-533.
LYNCH, M. E. (1985a) "Discipline and the material form of images: an analysis of scientific visibility." Social Studies of Science 15: 37-66.
LYNCH, M. E. (1985b) Art and Artifact in Laboratory Science. London: Routledge & Kegan Paul.
LYNCH, M., E. LIVINGSTON, and H. GARFINKEL (1983) "Temporal order in laboratory work," pp. 205-238 in K. Knorr and M. Mulkay (eds.) Science Observed. Newbury Park, CA: Sage.
MacKAY, R. (1974) "Standardized tests: objective/objectified measures of competence," pp. 143-217 in A. V. Cicourel et al., Language Use and School Performance. London: Academic Press.
MacKENZIE, D. (1978) "Statistical theory and social interests: a case study. Social Studies of Science 8: 35-83.
MAIMON, Z., A. RAVEH, and G. MOSHEIOV (1986) "Additional cautionary notes about the Pearson's correlation coefficient." Quality and Quantity: 1-13.
MAIMON, Z., I. VENESIA, and J. C. LINGOES (1980) "How similar are the different results?" Quality and Quantity 14: 727-742.
MARTIN, W. S. (1975) "The effects of scaling on the correlation coefficient." Journal of Marketing Research 10: 316-318.
MARTIN, W. S. (1978) "Effects of scaling on the correlation coefficient: additional considerations." Journal of Marketing Research 15: 304-308.
McCALL, G. J. and J. L. SIMMONS (1967) Issues in Participant Observation: A Text and Reader. Reading, MA: Addison-Wesley.
McCLOSKEY, D. N. (1985) The Rhetoric of Economics. Madison, WI: University of Wisconsin Press.
MEHAN, H. (1979) Learning Lessons: Social Organization in the Clasroom.
MEHAN, H. and H. WOOD (1975) The Reality of Ethnomethodology. New York: John Wiley.
MULKAY, M. (1984) "The ultimate compliment: a sociological analysis of ceremonial discourse." Sociology 18: 531-549.
MULKAY, M. and N. GILBERT (1983) "Scientists' theory talk." Canadian Journal of Sociology: 179-197.
NACHMIAS, D. and C. NACHMIAS (1976) Research Methods in the Social Sciences. New York: St. Martin's.
NORTON, B. J. (1978) "Karl Pearson and statistics: the social origins of scientific innovation." Social Studies of Science 8: 3-34.
O'BRIEN, R. M. (1979) "The use of Pearson's r with ordinal data." American Sociological Review 44: 851-857.
O'BRIEN, R. M. (1981a) "Using rank category variables to represent continuous variables: defects of common practice." Social Forces 59: 1149-1162.
O'BRIEN, R. M. (1981b) "Reducing grouping distortions in rank category variables." American Journal of Political Science 25: 605-616.
O'BRIEN, R. M. (1982) "Using rank order measures to represent continuous variables." Social Forces 61: 144-155.
PAWSON, R. (1982) "Desperate measures." British Journal of Sociology 33: 35-63.
REINHARZ, S. (1979) On Becoming a Social Scientist. San Francisco: Jossey-Bass.

ROTH, D. R. (1974) "Intelligence testing as a social activity," pp. 143-217 in A. V. Cicourel et al., Language Use and School Performance. New York: Academic Press.
RUDNER, R. S. (1966) Philosophy of Social Science. Englewood Cliffs, NJ: Prentice-Hall.
SACKS, H. (1963) "Sociological description." Berkeley Journal of Sociology 13: 1-16.
SCHEIN, E. (1985) Organizational Culture and Leadership. San Francisco: Jossey-Bass.
SCHWARTZ, H. and J. JACOBS (1979) Qualitative Sociology: A Method to the Madness. New York: Free Press.
SELLITZ, L. W. and S. COOK (1976) Research Methods in Social Relations. New York: Holt, Rinehart & Winston.
SILVERMAN, D. L. (1981) "The child as a social object: Down's Syndrome children in a pediatric cardiology clinic." Sociology of Health and Illness 3: 254-274.
SILVERMAN, D. L. and B. TORODE (1982) The Material Word: Some Theories of Language and Its Limits. London: Routledge & Kegan Paul.
SPEIER, M. (1973) How to Observe Face-to-Face Communication: A Sociological Introduction. Pacific Pallisades, CA: Goodyear.
SUDNOW, D. (1967) Passing On: The Social Organization of Dying. Englewood Cliffs, NJ: Prentice-Hall.
SUMMERS, G. F. (1970) Attitude Measurement. New York: Rand McNally.
THOREAU, H. D. (1985) Walden (original published in 1854). New York: Avenell.
TURNER, B. L. (1981) "Some practical aspects of qualitative data analysis: one way of organizing the cognitive processes associated with the generation of grounded theory." Quality and Quantity 15: 225-247.
TURNER, R. (1972) "Some formal properties of therapy talk," pp. 367-396 in D. Sudnow (ed.) Studies in Social Interaction. New York: Free Press.
Van MAANEN, J. (1973) "Observations on the making of policemen." Human Organization 2: 407-418.
Van MAANEN, J. (1978) "The asshole," in P. K. Manning and J. Van Maanen (eds.) Policing. Santa Monica, CA: Goodyear.
Van MAANEN, J. (1979) "Reclaiming qualitative methods for organizational research." Administrative Science Quarterly 24: 520-526.
Van MAANEN, J. (1982) "Fieldwork on the beat," pp. 103-151 in J. Van Maanen et al., Varieties of Qualitative Research. Newbury Park, CA: Sage.
Van MAANEN, J. (1983) "Golden passports: managerial socialization and graduate education." Review of Higher Education, 4: 435-455.
Van MAANEN, J. (forthcoming) Tales of the Field. Chicago: University of Chicago Press.
WINSHIP, C. and R. D. MARE (1984) "Regression models with ordinal variables." American Sociological Review 49: 512-525.
WOOLGAR, S. (1980) "Discovery logic and sequence in a scientific text ((1))," pp. 239-268 in K. D. Knorr et al. (eds.) The Social Process of Scientific Investigations. Sociology of the Sciences, Vol. IV. Dordrecht: D. Reidel.
WOOLGAR, S. (1981a) "Interests and explanation in the social study of science." Social Studies of Science 11: 365, 394.
WOOLGAR, S. (1981b) "Critique and criticism: two readings of ethnomethodology." Social Studies of Science 11: 504-514.
WOOLGAR, S. (1982) "Laboratory science: a comment on the state of the art." Social Studies of Science 12: 481-498.
YEARELEY, S. (1981) "Textual persuasion: the role of social accounting in the construction of scientific arguments." Philosophy of the Social Sciences 11: 409-435.

ABOUT THE AUTHOR

Robert P. Gephart, Jr., received his bachelor's degree in psychology with honors from Michigan State University, his master's degree in sociology from the University of Calgary, and his doctoral degree in commerce and business administration from the University of British Columbia. He joined the University of Alberta in 1979 and is currently Associate Professor in the Department of Organizational Analysis and Director of the Industrial Crisis Research Unit, Faculty of Business, University of Alberta, Edmonton, Alberta, Canada, T6G 2R6. In 1986, he was a Visiting Scholar in Organization Studies at the Sloan School of Management, Massachusetts Institute of Technology. His scholarly articles have appeared in a number of journals, including *Administrative Science Quarterly, Columbia Journal of World Business, Journal of Management, Qualitative Sociology,* and *Sociological Perspectives.* His recent (1987) book reviews have appeared in *Administrative Science Quarterly* and *Science.* In addition to ethnostatistics and research methods, his interests include ethnomethodology, organization theory, social studies of science, and the management of industrial crises. He is currently directing two major research projects concerned with the organizational basis of major industrial accidents and disasters, with funding from the Government of Alberta, Community and Occupational Health Division, and from the Social Sciences and Humanities Research Council of Canada.

ιJ